Psychoanalytic Reflections on Love and Sexuality

Gerd H. Fenchel

UNIVERSITY PRESS OF AMERICA,® INC.

Lanham • Boulder • New York • Toronto • Oxford

Copyright © 2006 by
University Press of America,® Inc.
4501 Forbes Boulevard
Suite 200
Lanham, Maryland 20706
UPA Acquisitions Department (301) 459-3366

PO Box 317
Oxford
OX2 9RU, UK

Library of Congress Control Number: 2005926389
ISBN 0-7618-3198-3 (paperback : alk. ppr.)
ISBN: 978-0-7618-3198-3

∞™ The paper used in this publication meets the minimum
requirements of American National Standard for Information
Sciences—Permanence of Paper for Printed Library Materials,
ANSI Z39.48—1992

Contents

Preface

Many treatises have been written on the mysteries and pain of love. Less has been written on the primitive nature of sexuality. Even less has been written on observations concerning the relation of both love and sexuality when they occur together, as they do, in every love affair, requited or not. It is true that on the subject of primitive sexuality, mythology has given us the god Dionysus celebrated over the centuries as the god of drunken orgies; and who has also not heard of Priapus and the Vestal Virgins? History is replete with even more creative literary works on the topic of romantic love. So has everything already been said on the topic of love and sexuality; and is there nothing new to be added?

During fifty-four years of clinical practice, I have encountered again and again friends and colleagues who have suffered unhappy or miserable love lives. Similarly, the majority of individuals coming into treatment are motivated and driven to do so by depression and romantic complaints resulting from unsuccessful relationships. Observing such unhappiness, I have been struck by how many men and women have complained of having been left by their partners. Before the bereft partner is able to "move on", the results of being left are usually devastating, the leaving partner making a new life while the one left behind remaining stuck and often inconsolable. Yet the breakdown of relationships has increased in our present day culture where an overly mobile and rootless society seems to exacerbate the process.

My observations have led me to two hypotheses. First, our culture is more turbulent today than twenty years ago; secondly, this seems to increase the need for some kind of stability in compensation, causing individuals to seek refuge in love affairs but which, unable to bear such unequalizing pressures, tend, more often than not, to end in disappointment. The old social mythology summed up in a Saturday Evening Post's portrait of two young people happy in love, married, settled down, raising a family, seems no longer to apply. More and more, people decide to remain childless, living together without being bound by either social or legal contract preferring, instead, to remain autonomous, individual and, though sharing time together as partners, remaining, nonetheless, free to follow, separately, the beat of a different drummer when the inclination arises. Ironically, then, it seems today that marriage is more a pre-occupation of the gay community (who see it as a badge of acceptance) than it is among the majority community of hetero-sexual couples. Is the gay community too, however, destined to be disappointed as well?

Besides my personal curiosity about our society, other factors stimulating this study include the effects of meetings held at Washington Square Institute during the years 1998 and 2000. Starting with the papers by Martin Bergmann, Charles Brenner and John Munder Ross, I began a study that took me back to ancient fable and Platonic myth and, after a long and complex path through classical and contemporary psychoanalytic literature, has led to these pages of observations and insights ending in the year 2004.

I was principally interested to reveal how much could be known about enduring relationships, to expose the stress points associated with such and to investigate how disaster could be circumvented. While engrossed in my research, I was haunted by the opposing views of Brenner and Bergmann; the latter confident that enduring relationships were possible with analysts, by their insights and facilitating therapeutic interventions, acting as "soldiers of Eros" while the former, more pessimistically, asserting that only swans mate for life. I leave it to the reader to decide. I hope only to have clarified the many and complex issues involved in deciding either more optimistically or more pessimistically the question of the viability of long lasting love relationships.

In all of this, I am indebted to my colleague and friend, Marc Angers, LCSW, who assisted not only in helping to craft the final conceptualization, but with whom I had many long conversations about philosophy, love and psychoanalysis. His breadth and depth of the subject viewed from different contexts helped to clarify many issues while our stimulating discussions impelled me to continue writing, covering more and more territory. So, for example, it was at his urging that I explored how love has crept into psychoanalysis under different guises and disguises.

Appreciation and thanks also go to my colleague and friend Kathleen Mays, Ph.D., who never tired in providing me with material I had not thought of. Last, but not least, I deeply appreciate the many secretarial services provided in this effort by Ms. Sondra Ospina.

Gerd H. Fenchel, Ph.D.

Introduction and Prelude

The search for our true nature follows many different paths. Knowledge about it has been inscripted in myths, the bible, philosophy, the arts and in popular convictions. None of these representations, however, contain the whole *picturem* which accounts for the diversity of so many contradictory accounts, stories and myths. Moreover, our thirst to know is counterbalanced by a strong resistance to know and acknowledge those features of ourselves that are the cause of disquiet or even abhorrence. Freud called attention to the fact that much of human nature is primitive and often at odds with the thin veneer of civilization that precariously overlays it. Indeed, how else to account for high divorce rates, violent crime and the seeming never ending situation of men at war with one another. Yet he also pointed out the need of mankind to strive for something better. Ideas of how to attain such a better life proliferate in such a rush of theories of meaning and moment that, in modern times, there often seems to be more confusion than clarity. Yet the world of possibility today is as much an artifact of our theories that construct it as are past thought and theory artifacts of constructions from the past.

The pace of change has had many effects upon our lives. It has weakened the strength of the nuclear family and, in so doing, undermined an important institution insulating each of us from the harsh realities of the world external to it. Moreover, in an extremely atomized society, it is difficult for individuals to create the sense of community necessary to support a sense of self in relation to others that promotes security, friendship and relatedness. With the supplanting of community by the logic of strategic advantage where each is out for himself, individuals have lost touch with their deeper human needs and are often left unhappy, lonely and anxious. Some turn to religion for comfort, hence the resurgence of fundamentalism. Where such comfort does not satisfy, others take refuge in the arts. Yet, at odds with our deeper natures as social beings needing meaningful relatedness in order to thrive, our age includes many who suffer from depression and find themselves in arid love relationships too often predicated upon physical titillation rather than upon a deeper intimacy. In such frustrating circumstances, many turn to drugs, alcohol and serial sexuality. These measures, however, only insure a deepening vicious circle.

More than ever, we need to rediscover the capacity to relate in more loving ways if we are to rescue ourselves from the oblivion of contemporary social reality. Yet, this thing called 'love' can either make us feel better about ourselves by connecting us deeply with another (or with others more generally), or it can disappoint and frustrate, throwing us into an abyss of depression and despair. Indeed, love is a passion that has always been seen as double edged, with the power to induce blissful happiness on the one hand or to toss us into a tumultuous agony on the other.

What follows, is an exploration of psychoanalytic observations on love and loving drawing upon myth, literature and poetry in an effort to reflect various ideas about passion and its vicissitudes at a certain point of time in history we call "the present." One of the early source books for such an investigation is the bible with its many stories of love and passion and all of the attendant iniquities and punishments following out of such passion. Even earlier myths such as the Nordic Veddas, the Indian Upanishads, Greek mythology and tribal initiation rites amplify our multi-leveled and multi-colored information about passion, love and death.

In this regard, perhaps the most enduring discussion of love occurs in Plato's *Symposium* where Plato presents a dialogue between Socrates and dinner guests about the nature of love. Of the various theories offered, two have remained in the imaginative consciousness of mankind (and, certainly, are both still alive today here in the West) in shaping our outlook on this most mysterious of human needs. The theory most often taken for granted by later generations comes from the speech of Aristophanes who proclaims (what is, perhaps, today linked with theories of narcissism), the view that once male and female parts existed in two headed creatures who were joined as one, but who, in angering Zeus, were split asunder and their once partnered parts scattered away from one another throughout the world thereby setting in motion the unhappy search on the part of each half for his or her other half. The second theory still ramifying in the cultural mythology of the West, comes from Socrates himself when he attempts to argue the position that love is a necessary condition for the examined life which is a necessary condition to having a life that is proper, as it were, to being a human being; the view, that is, that love is necessary for self-realization which is the process by which we become known to ourselves as human beings.

Yet "love" is also understood in our own contemporary culture in many other ways as well. What, for example, are people saying about sex these days? In our culture of unending adolescence, the word 'cool' might come to mind. Indeed, from high school on, certain views of life and certain practices are recommended, often, only on the weight of peer pressure implicit in the recommendation, 'cool.' Thus, it is 'cool' to play hard rock, to be hip, to pierce one's skin or to be tattooed. Many young girls, for example, look for sex or drug experiences to compete with their classmates while boys, too, seek drug experiences and accept dares in order to pass the tests of peer, adolescent rites of passage. These rites almost always include sexual experimentation for both boys and girls. Though much of this has always been the case in adolescence, many school psychologists today lament the increasing incidence of self-mutilation amongst teenagers. Others note with alarm the increase of teen suicide or of children turning on and shooting other children or their teachers. Meanwhile, our mental health centers are deluged by depressed men and women who seem to have given up on love and act out desperate and tragic scenarios as belated cries for help. Where, one might ask, has hope, love and the celebration of beauty gone in our lives?

In seeking an answer, we need to look to our culture and society and, more tellingly, perhaps, to psychoanalytic ideas illuminating the often inscrutable dynamics underlying such manifest structures. More profoundly, however, we need to understand the limits of love and sexuality in the context of classical and contemporary psychoanalytic theory if we are to be able to understand what is possible in any effort to ameliorate the conflicts afflicting ourselves and our society. In this we look to how some of these ideas have changed our relation to ourselves and, therefore, to the nature of our society itself.

For example, feminine liberation, while giving women the right to assert their fundamental equality, also had effects that deeply affected relationships between men and women. Then there were the 1960's that began a long process undoing the traditional authoritarian basis for the nuclear family. Meanwhile, economic pressures and social strivings created in the wake of rapid globalization reinforced the tendencies, already mentioned, in weakening lasting bonds of intimacy among individuals once held together by community modeled more on the organic ties of extended family rather than upon the impersonal forces of efficient production.

The once well defined and articulated social structure where each had a place, though in certain respects repressive, nonetheless supported a well defined sense of identity and role security for its members. Now, ill defined and heterogeneous, one's social identity is often defined by what one's immediate pragmatic goal is or what one's favorite product is. People move about from job to job and place to place giving society a nomadic and rootless quality. Moreover, the undoing of moral authority and the concomitant loosening of social structure has led to what others have called a culture of narcissism where, seemingly, each is out only for himself. Needless to say, bonds of intimacy under such a logic are, correspondingly, more difficult to sustain. Too many feel lost or isolated in a society where interconnections more and more seem to have become disjoined and individuals feel forced to cling to a false traditionalism on the one hand or, on the other hand, frantically search for modern solutions. As the tendency for such polarization becomes more marked, the center does not hold and we are left to wonder whether there exists any solution to right the imbalance.

Perhaps we need to learn to love again. Could it be that love is the answer, or by putting so much responsibility upon such a seemingly problematic and complex phenomena as love and loving, might we merely be moving from the frying pan into the fire? The answer, of course, will depend upon what we mean by 'love' and what understanding we can bring to such a perennial question. If this is too large a question for any one generation to attempt a definitive answer, then, perhaps we can at least offer a little light by considering what Sigmund Freud, one of the towering men of genius in our times, had to offer on the subject and what ramifications have followed in the wake of his ideas.

Chapter One

Love

WHAT'S LOVE GOT TO DO WITH IT?

There is a lot of confusion about the word 'love.' Quite possibly its meaning may not be fixed, but rather changes as time and culture change. In our culture love and hate are universally recognized as the strongest emotions that affect our emotional lives. Tracing its derivation, The Dictionary of Word Origins defines love as:

> Libidinous-strong desire-believing-and praise. The sense of pleasing is primary and associated with trust and believing. The derivation of love's sexual aspects is different and derives from lascivious currents connoting more primitive urges.

Over the years, various people have provided us with other definitions trying to capture the concept of love and to provide it with philosophical underpinnings. So, for example, Albert Schweitzer (1964), a deeply religious man, equated love with a certain reverential attitude towards the world and all living things. Love in this sense becomes a deeply inwardly reverberating spiritual experience that issues in action whereby the protection of life in all its variety is felt a moral good while destruction of life is felt as a moral evil. For Schweitzer, this universal ethic was held sacred. Though Schweitzer does not accept the idea of unconscious determinants governed by psychological principles, he does, nonetheless, believe that because progress is purchased at the expense of injuring others, we experience a sense of guilt in destroying life which requires, in compensation or as reparation, perhaps, the cultivation of a "reverence for life".

In contrast to the spiritual moralism of Schweitzer, who lived in Africa for many years and devoted his life to the welfare of others, Menninger (1964) and Fromm (1964) held to more psychologically grounded views of love. Nonetheless, Menninger also holds that the conditions of love are set within an economic system, but hopes that the cultivation of love can influence and change that system. Fromm, on the other hand, is concerned with character-habitual behavior traits and the views that condition them. In this, he contrasts what he considers the more romantic view of certain philosophers and poets on consequences to differences between the sexes with those whom he termed "reactionaries" and "existentialists" who, according to him, seem to say that there are no such differences between the sexes, only deficiencies. According to Fromm, the more romantic notion of sexual difference locates them in terms of trans-cultural biological and psychological givens and believes this idea is even reverberant in the interpretation of the sin committed by Adam and Eve in the Garden of Eden where God cursed Adam and Eve to ever after mutual conflict arising out of the "eternal" difference between their two sexes following the "fall".

Turning to his definition of 'love', Fromm (1964) explains that, although the character type of both sexes is determined mostly by their respective social roles following a process of socio-cultural socialization, nonetheless, he stresses as well the not insignificant fact that character type is also shaded by the differences inherent in sexual difference. Thus, noting that biology is destiny, because man's role in copulation is to penetrate and ejaculate into the woman's vagina, he suggests that the active organ is the phallus and the receptive organ is the vagina. Thus, he concludes, men, because their sex is more external and not easy to conceal (witness, for example, any erect penis), they tend to be more matter of fact and "up front" as it were with their sexuality while women, because their sex is more concealed, tend to be more reserved, and, perhaps more concealing of their feelings. Yet both are given to anxiety over feelings of vulnerability: the man, that he will not be able to perform and the women by feelings of dependency arising out of fear of abandonment. Each, of course, must desire the other: the man must feel he can satisfy her and she must feel she can satisfy him. She worries about her attractiveness and he about his physical prowess to command her attention. Thus both sexes share similar fears. Whether mutual attraction is to end in a positive experience, though, depends upon whether the whole character structures of the two lovers are as compatible as their sexual interest and desire.

As Reik (1964) sees it, the heart of the matter is that whereas sexual drive for a man and a woman may be undiscriminating since each needs only objects of opposite sex for sexual satisfaction, love, on the other hand, needs a subject. Thus, whereas 'sex' is primarily a biochemical (or physical) matter, 'love' is a psychological (or subjective) matter.

One cannot expect love to be a carbon copy of sex, in its very essence being the expression of the sexual drive. Love can exist before sexual desire is experienced and can outlast, often does in old age, the sexual appetite.

Following upon this distinction, George Bernard Shaw (1964) takes the view, with considerable empirical evidence to back it up, that no healthy man or animal is occupied with love for more than a brief time. Certainly marriage doesn't insure an ongoing sexual interest. If anything, he suggests, a good marriage depends more upon complementary habits and interests between the couple than upon ongoing sexual appetite for one another, an appetite that gets destroyed at the moment of gratification. More people, he thinks, if educated in this simple wisdom beforehand would be much happier after the fact if they could only come to grips with and accept this simple truth as a fact of life.

Now there are those, clergymen and educators, philosophers and writers who talk as if this can be prevented by taking a solemn (marriage) vow. In Shaw's ironical opinion, such people are either insincere or insane.

Taking us in a slightly different direction, but certainly not unrelated to the above, we can consider the ideas of 'love' stemming from a more scientific orientation such as that of Francis Bacon (1964) in contrast with the more philosophical views on the subject of the American philosopher George Santayana (1964). According to Bacon, love is the moving principle of the original corpuscles or atoms in motion and, as these are the building blocks of all matter including, therefore, human beings, mankind is driven by the force of love. Santayana, on the other hand, wants to start from the top and move down. He asks: 'what is ideal love'? He replies that love is at least half illusion: the lover, and not his love, is deceived by his madness; but his madness is 'divine'. Yet, because love is an emotion that enriches our lives, he thinks that not to believe in it would be to consign oneself to a life of dullness. He thinks the motive for our need to be in love arises in the first place from our need to dream about the people of whom we dream, and that such dreams contain the potentialities that prompt our desire. Everything that satisfies such desire reinforces the ideal, yet while the ideal is as constant as the nature it expresses, it doesn't itself exist nor can any apparent embodiment of it endure.

Rollo May (1964), an existential psychoanalyst, not surprisingly looks at the matter from the point of departure of an existential view point that contains many of the ideas we have considered thus far. For example, he repeats the idea that love is a rare and fragile phenomena and that it is rarely the sole reason for a long lasting relationship. He sees love as the delight one takes in the presence of the beloved with the consequent valuing of the other as much as oneself; yet he does not believe that love, in and of itself, can cure all the ills of the world. He underscores the fact that love presupposes freedom of choice and flourishes only in those with a capacity for independence. He notes, too, how love is tainted and corrupted by the superficial consumerism of our commercial economy—as though it can be bought and sold. Unlike the bargaining (or trading) motive underlying so much of our economic activity, he sees love as an end in itself that requires the maturity necessary for the capacity to give. It involves tenderness of heart and is probably embedded in Spinoza's definition of God, i.e. an unconditional loving that does not require "getting back".

The idea of freedom as intrinsic to love is profoundly underscored in the work of Ludwig Binswanger (1958), a precursor to the work of existentialist psychoanalyst Rollo May, who established a phenomenological version of what later became know as existential psychoanalysis. According to Binswanger, and following Heidegger's seminal magnum opus *Being and Time* (1962), the existential attitude requires giving up the attitude of mundane "facticity", of being a mere physical being existing in relation, merely, to a physical world. Rather, the existential attitude invites transcending the ordinary world of mere existence (ontic or factic orientation) for a more authentic subjective (ontological) immersion in experience, one oriented by the sense of dwelling, of "being there"(Da-sein), "in-the-world". (The categories of such "being-in-the-world" and their implications become the principle task of explication in Heidegger's *Being and Time,* the transcendental philosophy of Dasein, "being there".) Interestingly, from the existential standpoint of Da-sein, we learn that in the ontological orientation of "being-there in-the-world" there is no subject/object split as "being-in-the-world" is an attitude of transcendence that makes possible a sense of self-presence that, *thrown* into the world, as it were, creates the conditions for "authentic" experience, one that depends neither upon mere "ontic" or factual existence nor follows from any such "ontic" or factual circumstance. Dasein, in this sense, is governed by 'care' in relation to the horizon of "being-for-death", a reality calling for 'resolute' and 'authentic' "Being-for". . . , a condition of "freedom". On this view, 'love' is oriented in 'care' and 'care' presupposes authenticity, 'freedom'.

In a radical departure from such transcendental phenomenological moorings of 'love' and its equation to 'care' and caring in the 'ontological' sense of Heidegger and Binswanger above, we move from the sublime, let us say, to the rather less than sublime standpoint of the American psychoanalyst, Brenner (1998), who begins his musings on love by noting the not so surprising fact that love is accorded a special status in our culture. True enough. Indeed, as he points out, perhaps at no other time than our own nor in any other culture than ours, has love been placed as high upon an emotional hierarchy as in our own time and place. He notes that this particular sense of love, what he acknowledges as the rather common romantic sense of love we all share from countless cinematic and novelistic examples, can really only be traced back to the Minnesingers and troubadours of the 12th century when a broader notion of love, love outside marriage, was beginning to be recognized and, more importantly, celebrated for the first time in centuries. Indeed, before this time, the literature of past great civilizations, while mentioning 'love,' did not emphasize its importance quite the way we do in our times and culture. For example, Virgil gives it little importance; neither does Catullus or Ovid. While Persian poetry addresses love, Chinese poetry does not. Again, Brenner warns, "one must be at least somewhat cautious in attributing more than passing significance to what we take to have been the sources of the concept of 'romantic love' taken from the past" (p.113). Nor can the influence of religion be excluded from understanding the meaning of love.

While Jewish prophets and the psalms speak of love (indeed that one shall love God first and foremost), it is Christianity that takes the fore in developing a more complex notion of love by recalling the message of Jesus. Yet Brenner says, "eternal love, by which we mean love that lasts a lifetime, though possible, is not the invariable rule in human relations as it seems to be in other species, say, for example, as among swans" (p.114). Is Brenner's view jaundiced?

Where does one begin in attempting to sort out this immense question of 'love?' Do we need to reflect on evolutionary bio-psychology and what may have motivated Man during primitive times? Robert Gordon (2003) thinks so. He speculates that as a species we are unconsciously attracted to instinctive cues. Falling in love is a species-specific behavior that has survival value. Passion is based upon what is successful for individuals in the long run, not upon rationality per se (however "reasonable" such arrangements may turn out for the species in the long run). Primitive men sought youthful, attractive women since they were more likely to bear healthy offspring. Women, if they had a choice, were attracted to powerful men since they were more likely to be able to provide and to protect, and to pass on these qualities to their children. The passion of "pride" also enters here. Gordon says: "I have found that individuals who have little true understanding of mature love relations react more on this level than on a higher psychological level." Taking this line of thinking a step further, Helen Fischer (2004), an anthropologist, goes so far as to say that all romantic love stems from the need to reproduce the species. In her view, not only is there nothing mental or psychically determined in falling in love, but such relating is the effect merely of hard-wiring in the brains of human beings such that love is, fundamentally, really only a matter of neurobiology.

Bonaparte (1940) believes that the mysteries of life, love and death, and the fear of death may impel us to look for love. In a way reminiscent of Binswanger and Heidegger discussed above, Bonaparte notes that man is the only animal who is conscious of his finite life span. Animals lack this consciousness. On her view, the transformative power of love and lust stems from our animal heritage that allows us to moderate at times our existential fears. It is the identification with universal principles, indeed with the universe or cosmos in general, that gives humanity the capacity to be transformed by love (this because love links individual to cosmos).

> The humanity which I feel in face of the universe forces me to the conclusion that the human species has become attuned in the course of its long history to the environment to which it belongs and has evolved in complete harmony with it (p. 468).

Men have acquired the habit of dreaming in order to experience their lives as tolerable. Myths, legends and fairy tales represent the accumulated treasure of mankind. Pleasure in the intoxication of love is of limited duration. And since man cannot escape his ultimate destiny, he has tried, by transmitting his life to his work, sometimes at least, to survive through the creative achievements of his hands and brains. The power to survive belongs equally to the works of politicians, founders of religion, philosophers and scientists. Art and religion add another dimension to ameliorating the sense of man's common fate. It is true art that strikes a note of the eternal and universal in the human condition, giving a sense transcendence and the illusion, perhaps, of immortality. Yet, different races and religions have considerable variety in the sense in which life and death are experienced. Hindus and Chinese, for example, seem to live in a much more timeless world than Westerners and seem to have a greater apathy towards the question of death and the hereafter. The mystic projects his subjective feelings of eternity and in his imagination, perhaps, ascribes to it an objective existence.

According to Bonaparte, much of the death anxiety she speaks of can be traced back to the contrast between childhood where the world is untroubled by ideas of time and decay to the experience of time and decay in adulthood. The early days of childhood seem like an eternity to the child as do the years that stretch before them into the future. Then comes the period when adults impose their sense of time upon the child: when he is allowed to eat, sleep, and go to school; all this when he would rather continue just to enjoy himself in his reveries (pleasure). It is an intrusion upon the child of a strange and hostile world:

Perhaps the vital urge which causes him to grow, as it causes the plants to grow from the soil, and which will one day impel him in his turn to transmit life to an unbroken line of descendants, is already making itself obscurely felt from the depth of his being and is to be regarded as the factor which thus informs the child's sense of 'time' with a prescience of eternity (p. 427).

Even in adolescence, according to Bonaparte, time spreads out in a limitless expanse and, even with a notion of death, the adolescent does not believe it. The spirit of Eros takes possession of him with the feeling of infinity both as its essence and its aim. Death may seem to herald a transition to a coveted immortality, perhaps as in the fantasy of a form of unity with the great 'Mother'. Yet, in adult life, the grown-up may feel hampered by the slot he occupies and feel challenged in his assertive will to live.

In this struggle with time, Man employs the power of illusion. Dreaming and day-dreaming helps to create a magical atmosphere. Dreaming guards our illusions and we are transported out of our conventional lives back into the infantile time of childhood, a sort of paradise regained. We set about discovering states of mind analogous to those of our dream life even in our waking hours. As Santayana (1964) stated before in the above, in the power of dreams lies the greatness of love. Thus in all love is implicit the Faustian wish to recover one's youth; and it is Eros, through the aim of sexual love, that retrieves the aspect of life that is this immortality.

But Santayana also informs us about the contradictory nature of our wishes. Love from a biological point of view is confined to one period of life: in childhood we yearn for it but are not yet mature for it; in elderly years we may no longer feel equal to it and look back with regrets.

All of this seems to suggest that love, so centered as it seems in the repetition of infantile life, makes it just wishful thinking to suppose that one might also love and be in love with those qualities of the object of one's desire that are part of his or her personality and character in, as it were, the here and now as opposed to being a construction from the there and then. We will come to see, however as our story unfolds that these two aspects of love are not necessarily mutually exclusive. Indeed, sexual passions that later on may become fused with a certain type of love of the personal qualities of the beloved as a person may also reflect what we mean and hope to find in 'love'.

For now, though, and getting back to Gordon's position, one quite afar from the philosophical considerations we have been musing in terms of the relation of time, love and immortality, it is interesting to find echoed in none other than the poetry of Walt Whitman a position similar to Gordon's who, like Gordon, also underscores the power of evolutionary biopsychology as the force behind the momentous urge to procreation, an idea Whitman (1982) eloquently expresses in a fragment from the poem, *From Pent-up, Aching Rivers*.

In that particular passage, Whitman refers in song to a biological force-virility without which he would have no selfhood. He describes himself as very determined-even if he were 'sole among men.' He is jubilant feeling procreative forces or in his words 'singing the phallus' and attaches to this force the wish to procreate 'superb' children who will grow into 'superb' people.

Psychoanalytic theory, too, locates love in the force of instincts and drives. Whereas libidinal energy aims at fusion and attachment, aggressive energy tends toward separation and annihilation. Yet the passion of the drives cannot easily be equated with more romantic notions of love involving intimacy and mature dependence. In his seminal book (1987) and, later, in an important paper (1995), Martin Bergmann makes a helpful distinction in this regard when he distinguishes between "falling in love" and "staying in love." Yet, while Bergmann and Kernberg (1976) analyze the emotional processes between people, they do not address other kinds of love, e.g. love for one's country, or the arts, religion and the like.

The process of loving is unique. It regenerates the Ego and is a life force. It idealizes the loved object and in so doing increases our self-esteem and good feelings about ourselves. However, it is not always necessary for love to be directed towards another person for it to be experienced. We love beautiful scenery, a painting or sculpture, music and spirituality. Nor are these feelings necessarily based upon direct instinctual drives. Yet when we feel this way, we are taken out of our temporal and physical existence. We transcend ourselves and connect with idealized and illusionary objects seemingly on another, immaterial plane. Sometimes such connections to these transcendental "objects" may seem to possess the impelling force or quality of drive energy as, for example, the feelings we get when listening to the stirring strains of Beethoven's Ninth Symphony or upon hearing the Marseillaise or listening to Schumann's lieder. Yet other such objects are less impelling in this sense as, for example, the feelings we get when admiring a painting, looking at scenery or listening to less stirring music in which is evoked more a state of tranquility and harmony than the feeling of the force of a "drive."

The poet Wadsworth described it upon seeing daffodils.

In reverie lying on a couch, he may not think of anything or he may be preoccupied, there appears the picture of daffodils swaying in the breeze and fills him with a feeling of supreme bliss.

But no matter whatever state of love we may be in at the moment, whether we feel driven or tranquil, there is a common thread of transcendence of the self in all such experiences; a seeking to connect with others in confirmation (or consummation) of this basic common experience (need). When experiencing such a consummation of our need to love, we no longer feel isolated, but are connected with something larger than ourselves. Interestingly, much of this process involves the use of, and therefore the capacity for using, symbols and symbolization of which we shall say more presently.

DIFFERENT KINDS OF LOVE

Having spoken above of some of the general features of love, let us now turn to considering some of the different kinds of love. To begin, let us consider the love one may feel for one's country. First of all, it is worth noting that love for one's country or ethnic group need not necessarily imply ethnocentrism. Yet many people love their country or ethnic group and are grateful for what they derive from them. The more satisfied people are in their identification with their country, the greater, often, the individual and collective morale. For example, during the Carter administration national morale was quite low. We were ashamed and disheartened not only by Vietnam, but, more disturbingly, by what appeared as impotence to resolve the hostage crisis in Iran. With national morale and identity at such low levels, patriotism seemed empty and was even frowned upon. With the advent of a new president, however, and a resolution of the hostage crisis, the memory of Vietnam began to be overtaken by a resurgence of national pride. We were no longer ashamed of ourselves and marching bands seemed to herald a new day, one which proclaimed the message: "I am proud to be an American!"

However, such love and pride in one's country or group can have many salutary effects beyond mere bombast. For example, since the Holocaust it has often been lamented that it was as if the Jews of Europe suffered passively their extermination. Yet, during these desperate years, isolated by the rest of the world and seemingly, thereby, powerless, they were alone. Shunned, seemingly, even by the non-fascist powers, and with no place to turn, such rejection, on top of unspeakable cruelty for no other crime than their mere existence, may have fostered in the hearts of Europe's Jews a sense of shame as much as of outrage. In any case, against such odds, pride had to be sacrificed to what ever it took merely to survive. This did not mean, however, that the Jews murdered in Europe, while the rest of the world looked on, went to their deaths as so many sheep to slaughter. History since the holocaust has proven differently. Indeed, when given a chance, after an heroic struggle, the birth of

Israel and its recognition by the United Nations established a nation of proud fighting Jews in a place that had special meaning for them in a line of succession that could be traced back from generation to generation to biblical times. Experienced by him as his rightful due from a world that had so callously permitted his people to be exterminated, today's Israeli Jew is determined that "never again" be not only a rhetorical slogan, but an ongoing act of foreign policy backed by military might and steadfast determination to survive at all costs.

Such feelings of non-exaggerated pride in the group by which and through which one identifies are important to feeling good and secure in one's existence. There is an implied belongingness beyond oneself to others that creates an optimistic outlook and hope for the future. While affiliation with a group larger than oneself strengthens the ego and raises self-esteem, it also preserves individuality. Such uniqueness in belonging is echoed by our Founding Fathers who struggled to satisfy diverse needs by forging a common path expressed so eloquently in the Declaration of Independence and our Constitution. (Interestingly, this process of needing to find commonality in difference operates not only in larger groups but also among couples.)

In another domain, and on a slightly different tack, we notice that religious feelings, loving "God," are often confused with the teachings of organized, ritualized religion. Such organizations represent the institutionalization of religious feeling into codes of ritualistic behavior. In such objectifications, the love of "God," the whole point of the ritual, is sometimes lost as the ritual begins to take over in importance. A good example can be found in the Jewish religion. Indeed, historians believe that monotheism, while representing a higher moral development replacing with strict ritual codes the looser more polymorphous polytheism that preceded it, nonetheless, did not further the spirit of the love of "God" even though it preserved the group. Had it embodied a deeper sense of that love, there would not have been the need for such strict and punitive enforcement of codes, since a corollary to such deep experiences of love is a tendency for compassion and fellow feeling for one's neighbor, feelings at odds with such brutal enforcement codes. Indeed, an eye for an eye and a tooth for a tooth, or the stoning to death of a supposed adulteress, do not attest to a society built upon the fellow feeling that arises naturally from compassionate love. Yet such barbarous practices continue to this day in some African countries and among certain fundamentalist followers of Islam. In contrast, and more in line with the sort of compassionate love celebrated in certain oriental philosophies such as Buddhism, the goal of enlightened living is an inner peace and harmony with one's self and with one's natural environment.

Love of "God" and "Man" is more likely to be found in non-codified religious traditions. Jewish mysticism developed as a reaction to the strict rabbinical interpretations of the Ten Commandments. (So did Christianity.) The concepts of law and justice, so prevalent in the Old Testament, were replaced with love and forgiveness in the New Testament. In the mystical book, the Kabbalah, "God" is described as imperfect, almost like a moody child. He is at once loving and forgiving; angry and punishing. The book says that Man was created to help "God" with his imperfections and to reestablish harmony amongst body, soul and world. "Man," by his good deeds, creates the more perfect world. Love, forgiveness and harmony are the goal. The inexplicable and unforgivable are explained and forgiven. "Man" must forgive "God" for the Holocaust and, in so doing, add to divine harmony. (This example reminds us of the analytic process whereby patients have to forgive their parents, i.e., work through their negative parental introjects, in order to be at peace as adults.)

Jewish folk tales describe "Man" as having a very personal relationship with "God." Jews pray to "Him," complain to "Him," love "Him" and are angry at "Him." *Fiddler on the Roof* is a good example of this idea. Such dialogue continues in houses of worship where we observe congregants praying with emotional fervor while swaying to melodies remembered since childhood. Such worshippers transcend their ordinary lives. Their petty jealousies and annoyances are left behind and their hearts are filled with love and an inner harmony.

In our materialistic culture, emphasis on the spirit is practiced by the counter-culture. The idea of loving is very important. It may be expressed by alcohol or drug orgies or in the exhibitionism of Hollywood movies . It may also be expressed in the teachings of gurus or yogis. Nor, because our culture breeds loneliness, can we discount such attempts to find the feeling of love through the use of alternative medicines.

Our society, unfortunately, both promotes and reinforces attempts at narcissistic compensations for inner emptiness. The problem with such narcissistic cures, however, as previously stated (Fenchel, 1994a), is that they can attain to only temporary and fleeting harmony until the real world reasserts itself. One such narcissistic solution, the idea of narcissistic compensatory loving, was prominent in the underlying dynamics practiced by some encounter group movements in the 1980's. Many more examples abound.

Turning now to the arts, we know that feelings of love are evinced in the presence of the beauty of a painting or sculpture; in beautiful music or literature, all of which contributes to a libidinal sense of self loving in a state of inner harmony. Have we not stood transfixed in front of the Pieta, Moses or the Thinker; have we not viewed the Mona Lisa or the paintings of the Old Masters and experienced a sense of satisfaction and awe? The sculptured lines, the vibrant colors preserved through the ages, the composition and exquisite detail—all evoke admiration and connect us to what the artist wanted to convey.

Has love not been celebrated in stories and poetry for many generations? Even early on during our school days as children and young adults, have we not been imbued with the ideals of love sung so eloquently by the poets? Who, for example, cannot recall Elizabeth Barrett Browning's (1982) declaration of love in the following lines:

> How do I love thee? Let me count the ways
> I love thee to the depth and breadth and height
> my soul can reach . . . (p. 112).

Or Christopher Marlowe's (1982) passionate shepherd in:

> Come live with me and be my Love
> and we will all the pleasures prove
> that hills and valleys, dales and fields
> or woods of steep mountain yield . . . (p. 67).

Similar emotions are stimulated by musical compositions. Schlachet & Waxenberg (1988) show that different conceptions of love are also found in popular ballads. Classical pieces by Bach, Beethoven or Brahms also help us to transcend ourselves as they transport us with their melody and harmonies into the music of our souls. In contrast, today's music seems less often to produce such feelings of transcendence as it reflects more the merely solipsistic narcissism of the culture of narcissism. Yet, optimistically, perhaps, Schlachet and Waxenberg observe a backlash. Indeed, according to these authors "We speculate that the renewed interest in enduring love is a backlash against a culture of narcissism and consumption that emphasizes the primacy of the individual over the human need to relate in an interdependent way, which leaves its members feeling empty and alienated with nothing but the quick fix of a new sensation to provide temporary comfort" (p.61). The mood of this culture is succinctly described in Leonard Bernstein's (1997) *Mass*:

> What I say, I don't feel
> What I feel, I don't show
> What I show, isn't real
> What is real, Lord, I don't know (p. 30).

THE ESSENCE OF LOVE

Having discussed these various forms of love, the question may arise as to what, if anything, do they have in common. Perhaps Brenner (1998) is correct when he admonishes that love is not a noun; that it describes behavior. But surely we also have to look beneath the behavior, to the inside, as it were, of what we experience in loving in order to grasp the inner nature of such behavior. In the above examples, we noted the quality of transcendence from the temporal and corporal aspects of existence. We noted that when experiencing love we seem to leave behind day to day differences and our narcissistic selves and seem to experience a sense of inner peace and connectedness with something beyond ourselves; we are transformed in the moment and experience a kind of peace that, for some, is akin to the sense one has when in a deep meditation. We are restored to ourselves and, if we are lucky, perhaps even changed in the way we see, or look at, the world.

Such deeply restorative experiences that love in this sense provides, has helped the terminally ill to survive; to stay alive. Yet in a certain sense, we are all terminally ill, for the destination of each of us is death; but when we experience love, or live a life rich in loving, we are in touch with, and touched by, something deeply infused with life and living; something deeply at odds with death and dying. Again, when we love, we are restored to ourselves and can tolerate the petty disappointments of life; its traumas and bitterness. We become, in Bergman's words, "soldiers of Eros," armed with a life force that is profoundly libidinal.

Interestingly, psychoanalytic opinions are divided about love. Reik (1944) insisted that sex and love were not the same and that ego functions played a larger role than instincts. There are many analysts who agree. Reik also believed that love was a reaction formation against hate, envy and jealousy. Brenner (1998) called it "compromise formation." Fromm (1956) saw love as a healthy separateness—an existential phenomenon not related to instincts while Rollo May and Binswanger view separate-ness as bound up in the existential categories of 'authenticity' and 'freedom'. In addition, and in their own ways, both Santayana and Bonaparte raise the interesting question of whether love can ever be more than an illusion out of dreams (Santayana) or out of the impulse to repeat infantile fantasy (Bonaparte). As we continue in our exploration of 'love,' we will have to see which, if any of these formulations, best reflects its nature. However, for the time being, let us move on to consider 'love' and its relation to the complex problem of symbolization.

LOVE AND SYMBOLIZATION

Our life is governed by symbols that evoke certain affects. For instance, tachistocopic experiments show that flash cards inscribed with the words "mother," "love," etc. often provoke in the subjects before whom they flash, feelings of bliss and physiologically induced states of serenity. As early as 1905, Freud stated that the capacity for symbolic formation by the mind was a normal feature of "mindedness" as it were and was not necessarily an outcome of repression. Susan Deri (1984), attempting to expand psychoanalytic metapsychology, defined symbols as designating something "absent." She viewed symbol-making as an innate capacity of the mind giving a sense of order and connectedness within the psyche as well as promoting bridging from the inside to the outside.

Bergmann (2002) cogently remarks that during psychoanalysis we translate from the pre-verbal realm to the realm constructed out of words. Moreover, it has been a tenet of psychoanalytic wisdom since its inception to notice that when chaotic unconscious wishes are put under the dominion of words, they become accessible to the Ego; and the effects of symbolization in this sense create the conditions for the possibility by which the psyche is anchored in reality. Through symbols we gain distance from raw experience through the ego's capacity for self-observation and affect regulation. Interestingly, but not surprising, then, is the fact that when the relationship between the symbol and what it represents becomes impaired, so too is impaired the quality of reality relatedness by the perceiver.

De-symbolization can occur as an extreme defensive measure—or may point to faulty ego development. Lack of normal symbolization can create a condition of mind where thoughts are concrete where, as it were, the word is the thing. So too, in such circumstances, the self becomes experienced as thing-like and concrete. Symbolization, then, is an essential condition for normal self-experience and perception. In psychoanalysis, items at different levels of mind dissociated by pathological defenses become linked through the process of analysis where one is recovered as representation of another in a process of ever increasing psychic integration. Thus, the capacity for symbolization is a necessary condition to recovering psychic health where experience becomes ever more coordinated via symbolization.

Yet, symbolization is not inborn. The infant needs the loving help and nurture of those surrounding him in order to develop this capacity. The capacity to achieve symbolization, however, can be adversely affected if the infant is overwhelmed by overly strong affects in the early stages of its development. It needs a "good enough" maternal environment if the process of symbolization is to take root.

Now, by the same token that the unconscious is organized by the reality oriented function of symbolization, so, too, the symbolizing structure of language reveals the unconscious. The two realms of conscious and unconscious are preserved by the symbol, as it were, in a sort of dialectical unity. And, as Bergmann points out, the need for gratification of sexual and aggressive drive discharge is focused by, and at the same time contained in, the ego structure facilitated as it is by the role that symbolization plays in, as it were, the taming of the drives. For, above all, the function of symbolization is to give us some distance, via abstraction, from these intense drive derivatives. Indeed, when those who experience their thoughts and experiences so strongly that their capacity to have distance from them is impaired, the results can be very disruptive:

> Strong emotions, whether sexual or aggressive, tend to interfere with the capacity to differentiate the symbol from what is symbolized. When that happens, the patient loses the capacity to know that the analyst stands for father or mother, representing the figures of childhood, but is not at the same time identical with them (p.24).

As we have seen, the psychoanalytic concept of symbol formation, related as it is to the dual instinct theory, suggests interesting clinical applications as well. Because symbols serve a libidinal, and therefore "containing" and organizing function, people who are primarily organized by aggressive drive derivatives have difficulty in their capacity to be reality oriented. They also have difficulty in loving. Intense hate, like the death instinct, follows the principle of inertia under which life stagnates or disintegrates. As observed in depressed patients (Fenchel, 2004), such individuals are not able to fully participate in life but, drawn instead to past disappointments and failures, are veiled in tragic and moody affect. In psychoanalytic parlance, we might say of such persons that they are possessed of greater character pathology.

Ego building requires a preponderance of libido. Once properly formed and integrated, the ego serves as an important synthesizing capacity of the psyche enabling it to overcome the tendency for splitting and disintegration fueled by the pressure of more aggressive and disorganizing tendencies of mind. And it is the capacity for symbolization that best facilitates this synthetic capacity of a well functioning ego. Symbols provide a means of crossing over boundaries and of healing splits. They bind energy and transform power—they are energy regulators. They delay immediate, narcissistic gratification and further secondary process. While they connect and transcend, they also create the conditions for the possibility of both individuation and separateness.

So much of the topic of symbolization hinges upon the way language and the capacity for language links the inner impulse with outer reality. Language, as it were, binds impulse, affect idea and reference to an object all in the "act" of symbolization. The theoretical implications for this phenomenon are enormous and, recently, formed an extended discussion by Theodore Shapiro (2004) who sees it not only as the basis for a theory of symbolization, but also as the link between a neural-cognitive model of mind on the one hand and intra-subjective and intersubjective psychoanalytic models of mind on the other. He points out that in the 21st century, psychoanalytic theories of mind continue to employ models that depend upon mentalization viewed from two angles: neural inhibition on the one hand and emergent constructions out of social discourse in an intersubjective field on the other. Moreover, in noting the recent focus upon enactments, intersubjectivity and social constructivism and their possible relationship to the findings in neuro-imaging and cognitive neuroscience, he is heartened that Freud's holistic hope for a comprehensive science of human beings might be achieved through an understanding of drives from a biological standpoint in relation to a psychology of mind seen from the standpoint of being an emergent property of social-cultural narratives implicit in the developmental potential of mature mindedness (self-conscious awareness).

As such, language is seen as the bridge between body and mind and as between persons. The idea is that language is a function of the mind's propensity to modulate the reflex arc of stimulus-response events. The mediation process is what psychoanalysis studies in the form of personally constructed meaning units. The coding of meaning is perforce in language and, moreover, it is via words that psychoanalysts interpret meaning to their patients. Thus the words of the patient in the context of the interpretive words of the psychoanalyst are reinternalized by the patient and go to re-code the neural patterns formed in the arc of those stimulus response events that patterned neural inhibition. Neural inhibition is replaced by neural transference to neural discharge. In understanding this process, "we need to translate other methodological shibboleths such as empathy, intersubjectivity and unconscious communication" (p.349) into meaningful new mechanisms for processes, as yet unknown, that guide thought and action. Just as love will never be reduced to mere chemical co-occurrences (nor to its merely neural discharge of bold affect), so too, the word is neither the thing nor the experience itself, but, rather, the mediating symbol that makes both possible. In the absence of any other possibility, human communication, internal monologue and dialogue are dependent upon the symbolic capacity inherent in the capacity to form and express experience in words.

Now, discussing the process of symbolization and the implications it has on the capacity to use words and what that suggests about the way the mind develops in relation to its goal of greater and greater reality orientation (while preserving and reinforcing integration and structure) is one thing, while discussion of the effects that specific symbols can have on the mind is another.

The latter are mediated by the influence of culture and so involve meanings both conscious and unconscious by which the culture is constituted and in terms of which individual psyches are situated. Culture, through its values, mores, customs and taboos related to the regulation of sexuality, reinforces strictures first encountered in the unique family experiencethat each individual internalizes in the formation of his or her psychosexuality. This experience, as we know, is rife with conflict. Thus, culture, experienced both as constraint as well as well as an arena for fantasies of liberation, reinforces ambivalence, but also, for the reasons just stated, has the potential to trigger intrapsychic conflict. The outcome of such conflict may be disintegrative depending upon whether what is activated can be contained by the particular psyche without diffusion of structural integrity. The latter weakens the ego in its capacity to bind (by neutralizing or sublimating) aggressive and libidinal drive derivatives (meaning drives).

Thus, in the hands of clever minds bent on manipulating other minds, symbols in this sense can be used for good or bad effect. Dictators use symbols for manipulation of others. Inflammatory oratory can arouse people to commit unthinkable deeds (inside and outside). The use of symbols by pathological people can have an effect upon a group no different from the way pathology in the individual can disorganize and undermine its unity and reality oriented capacities. Symbols in this sense can powerfully influence the seeming intractableness of neurotic fixation. Yet by pointing out this aspect of the disorganizing effects that certain symbols can have on the psyche, we by no means contradict the thesis that the process of symbolization plays an important synthetic function in organizing and structuring the mind; and that this process is an expression of the life-force, Eros, in its capacity to create the conditions for the possibility of a thirst for a life of love and living. Symbolization in this sense helps us to come to grips with (while we live under the shadow of) the inevitable fact of our human mortality. This fact also bespeaks of why we have such a basic need for illusion and transcendence, the objects in terms of which such feelings are aroused being, presumably, as varied from person to person as each individual is unique in personal history.

REFERENCES

Bacon, F. The myth of cupid. In: *The World of Love. V. 1.* (Ed) I. Schneider, p. 21–23. New York: George Braziller, 1964.

Bernstein, L. (1997) *Mass.* New York: Sony, SM2K 63089.

Binswanger, L. The existential analytic school of thought. In: *Existence* (ed.) R. May, p. 191–213. New York: Basic Books, 1958.

Bonaparte, M. (1940) Time and the unconscious. *International Journal of Psycho-Analysis, 21:*427–468.

Bergmann, M. (1987) *The Anatomy of Loving.* New York: Columbia University Press.

——. (1995) On love and its enemies. *Psychoanalytic Review, 82:*1–19.

——. (2002) The symbolic and the real in the therapeutic relationship. *Issues in Psychoanalytic Psychology,24:*11–25.

Brenner, C. (1998) Thoughts on love and hate. *Issues in Psychoanalytic Psychology, 20:*113–121.

Browning, E. B. How do I love thee. In: *Love: A Celebration of Art & Literature.* (ed.) Jane Lahr and Lena Tabori, p. 112. New York: Stewart, Tabori & Chaing Publishers, 1982.

Deri, S. (1984) *Symbolization and Creativity.* New York: International Universities Press.

Fischer, H. (2004) Why Do We Love? New York: Henry Holt & Co.

Fenchel, G. (1994a) Religion and spirituality. In: Fenchel (ed.), *Psychoanalysis at 100.* Maryland: University Press of America.

——. (1994) Love and hate in narcissistic pathology: techniques for the therapist and the group. *Issues in Psychoanalytic Psychology,16:*181–190.

——. (2003) To Be or Not to Be—that is the question. Depressed Affect Revisited: causes, dynamics and treatment. *Issues in Psychoanalytic Psychology,(in press).*

French, T. & Fromm, E. (1964) *Dream Interpretation: A New Approach.* New York: Basic Books.

Fromm, E. Sex and character. In: *The World of Love. V. 2,* (ed.) I Schneider, p. 192–205. New York: George Braziller, 1964.

Gordon, R. (2003) Personal communication.

Heidegger, M. (1962) *Being and Time.* New York: Harper & Row.

Kernberg, O. (1989) Aggression and love in the relationship of the couple. *Journal of the American Psychoanalytic Association, 39:*45–70.

Marlowe, C. The passionate shepherd to his love. In: *Love: A Celebration of Art & Literature,* (ed.) Jane Lahr and Lena Tabori, p. 67. New York: Stewart, Tabori & Chaing Publishers, 1982.

May, R. A preface to love. In: *The World of Love. V. 2,* (ed.) I. Schneider, p. 279–281. New York: George Braziller, 1964.

Menninger, K. Love against hate, In: *The World of Love. V. 2,* (ed.) I. Schneider, p. 5–32. New York: George Braziller, 1964.

Reik, T. (1944) *A Psychologist Looks at Love.* New York: Farrar & Rinehart.

——. (1964) Love and sexuality. In: *The World of Love. V. 2,* (ed.) I. Schneider, p. 310–317. New York: George Braziller, 1964.

Santayana, G. Ideal love. In: *The World of Love. V.2,* (ed.) I. Schneider, p. 137–154. New York: George Braziller, 1964.

Schlachet,B. & Waxenberg, B. (1988) What is this thing called love? The popular ballad as a framework for changing conceptions of love. In: Lasky & Silverman (eds.), *Love-Psychoanalytic Perspectives,* 52–62. New York: New York University Press.

Schweitzer, A. Reverence for life. In: *The World of Love. V.2,* (ed.) I. Schneider. p. 2–24. New York: George Braziller, 1964.

Shapiro, T. (2004) Use your words. *Journal of the American Psychoanalytic Association 52*:331–353.

Shaw, G.B. Preface to getting married. In: *The World of Love. V. 2,* (ed.) I. Shneider. p. 435–447. New York: George Braziller, 1964.

Whitman, W. From Pent-up, Aching Rivers. In: *Love: A Celebration of Art & Literature,* (ed.) Jane Lahr and Lena Tabori, p. 110–111. New York: Stewart, Tabori & Chaing Publishers, 1982.

Chapter Two

Freud on Love

FREUD'S CONTRIBUTIONS

Freudian tradition places love at the center of its theoretical formulations. The basic dynamic is explained in terms of the idea that in "love," the libidinal drive undergoes sublimation and is deflected from its direct sexual aims. The vicissitudes involved in the transformation of the drive in this sense, especially as a response to developmental imperatives and constraints experienced during the formative years of life, is what determines the quality of love for any given person reaching the stage of adult maturity. Romantic love of the more adult phase of life has the potential for adding a new dimension to the drive— consciousness of a concern, as it were, for something other than the self, namely, attraction and concern for the unique qualities of the beloved other. Yet, according to Shuren (1975), a complex emotional relationship that contains both physical and emotional satisfaction obtained in close association with the love object is rare. This split between the capacity to conjoin both sexual and affective currents in the person of one beloved object was perceived by Freud as arising out of the effects of the complex of the incest taboo upon the psyche of the lover. Indeed, according to Freud, the fact of such splitting is considered quite common an outcome for most would be lovers, since there are so many obstacles disrupting and obstructing the path to the integration of instinctual drive with ego 'drive.'

Freud's thinking on love covers the areas of attachment and sexual bonding. He emphasized in all of his writings that love relationships were not accidental but, rather, were the outcomes of the necessary search each must make in order to find a substitute for the felt loss of an earlier lost love object. The nature of the attachment to this early lost love object, 'the mother,' and the degree of successful separation from her will determine the degree to which we are successful in finding a substitute that is gratifying of both sexual and affectionate currents in our need to love. If we are not sufficiently separated from her, that is, if there has been a fixation in our developmental road leading out of infantile life, our capacity for gratification of both sexual and affectionate currents with a substitute, age appropriate, love object will be seriously undermined.

Even when all is working well in love, however, such relationships may not be permanent. Indeed, in successful love relations where the woman's sexual integrity is prized and reciprocated by the lover's faithfulness and fidelity; nonetheless, as with the waning of the sense of the excitement in the discovery of "the new," so too, often, is there a waning in the sense of commitment to the relationship. Eventually, yielding to the inevitable pressures of disillusion and disconnect (especially sexual) brought about by such waning passion, there is a break-up of the old relationship followed by the finding of a new one that is once again charged with the passion of new found love. Moreover, this process may be repeated many times over the course of one's erotic life.

According to Freud, as already mentioned, the subtle forces undermining successful love are consequent to its genesis in infantile life. For example, many a frequent attachment is made to a woman who is not unattached. At the same time, jealousy and desirability increase with women who are more or less sexually discredited, whose fidelity and loyalty admit of some doubt. The compelling force to love such a possible love object is sometimes characterized as the force of "love as rescue," where the love object is felt especially in need of rescue by a new, superior lover. The injured "third party" (the husband or boyfriend), however, often, and quite naturally, feels great enmity to such intruding, competing rivals. Yet in all of these relationships (degrees of which are also found in normal love), the complicating desirability of the not unattached, but 'fallen,' women is driven by some degree of fixation derived from the sensation of tenderness for the mother, the first love object, and represents one of the forms in which the fixation expresses itself in adult life.

While, under normal conditions, this fixation, though complicating things, is but a thin shadow cast over the love life of the adult psyche of a more integrated ego, in other instances, where regression plays a more significant role, a more dramatic re-enactment of the earlier love relationship with the mother takes place. In such instances where, under the influence of more dramatic fixation, one's choice of love object is focused by a more straight forwardly undisguised mother surrogate, things get more complicated and the injured third party becomes felt as an actual oedipal rival. In

such circumstances where the old childhood struggle with the father is re-
joined in the adult love relationship with the mother surrogate, loving becomes seriously interrupted by the ensuing conflict. Freud (1910) put it
this way:

> The pressing desire in the unconscious for some irreplaceable thing often re-
> solves itself into an endless series in actuality—endless for the very reason that
> the satisfaction longed for is, in spite of all, never found in any surrogate
> (p.197).

Examining psychic impotence, Freud (1912) came to the conclusion that
the erotic instinct and tenderness need to combine for a successful union.
Where incestuous fixations have not been overcome, erotic life remains dissociated: "Where such men love they have no desire and where they desire
they cannot love" (p.207). The idealization of the woman prevents the more
animalistic sexual passion to be expressed. For such passion to be expressed,
the woman must be degraded in the mind of the lusting lover. But even then,
owing to the strength of repression of a sexual impulse too closely associated
with the actual mother (the mother of fixation), the sexual act may be performed without pleasure.

The moral is that the person who wants to be really free and happy in love
must have overcome his or her deference for the opposite sex, rooted in over
idealization, and to have come to terms with his or her own incestuous fantasies. But even then, Freud cautions that the mature sexual instinct may not
be performed with pleasure if there is too strong a connection between the animalistic organs of orgasm and those of excrement; for such conflation leads
to sexual inhibitions. Here, perhaps, the cultural necessity of sublimation (and
reaction formation) tends to work against absolute gratification.

Regarding freedom to engage in erotic sexuality, Freud concentrated on
factors that he felt were inherent in women inhibiting such freedom. According to Freud, in order to surrender virginity, the lover needs to overcome the
influence of education. Defloration is experienced as a narcissistic wound and
the fantasy of diminished sexual value. The loss of virginity, then, is associated in women the loss of sexual attractiveness, the effect of which can be an
inhibition of sexual interest and some enmity towards the deflowering lover.
A second factor generating some enmity toward the lover is the fact that a
woman's first choice is her father, the husband or lover being, at best, only a
second hand replacement. In some cases, too, the feelings of penis envy may
also serve as a resistance and source of enmity.

If, however, the woman surrenders to her lover and feels gratified by his at-
tentions and tenderness, the condition of "thralldom" can develop. Thralldom
develops in a sexual relationship when the person loses the sense of indepen-

dence and may feel the urge to sacrifice personal interests to those of her lover (Freud, 1918). When this takes place, it binds the woman and the man together closely in an erotic relationship that frees the woman from the inhibiting archaic reactions toward the man described above. In pathological forms, women who are utterly alienated from their husbands still cling to them but no longer with affection: "They cannot free themselves from him because their revenge upon him is not yet complete" (p.235).

Freud appears to be saying that a good love relationship is hard to find. The couple has to work against cultural inhibitions. The man must be able to combine affection with eroticism and enable the woman to overcome (a) her father fixation, (b) her enmity about losing independence and (c) her devalued feelings in no longer being a virgin. For the man to achieve the conditions for the possibility for such passionate relationships, he must primarily master, by overcoming, his fear of incest. But even if all conditions are fulfilled, according to Freud, absolute gratification is never completely attainable and the best one can hope for is a "good enough" relationship with a prevailing manifest current of sexual passion.

According to Freud, it is the goal of civilization to modify (sublimate) the nature of direct physical sexuality into a concern for the goals of society. When contrasted with the more primitive goals of direct sexual satisfaction, this pressure to sublimate may lead to a rather painful dilemma; for the pressure to sublimate is often felt as a pressure to repress. Unlike Freud, however, Shuren (1975) does not emphasize this repressive force of society as being linked as the cause of our sexual ills. He does not believe that we need more love but rather poses the thought that we need more concerned people who are able to love. According to Shuren love, in and of itself, is rooted narcissistically, yet shows itself in intense concern. When a child feels such intense concern for itself by a loving parent, it's narcissism is gratified and creates in the child an intense zest for life:

> That zest for living is what I see as a precondition for love, a love which can be modulated and made durable through moderation and humility (p.25).

What Shuren adds to Freud's theory of instincts is a theory of attachment and the focus of an object oriented dimension of concern intrinsic to the passion of loving. According to Shuren, the inability to sustain an integrated sense of self in so many of today's children is laid at the doorstep of parents who are deficient in showing their children the requisite sense of concern to fuel their independence and sense of zest for living. Because these parents have shown their children such lack of genuine concern and physical gratification, it may be difficult to convince such children in treatment that they should want more from life.

Stephen A. Mitchell (2002), the late distinguished relational theorist, offers another slant on the complexities of loving. In our discussion in this chapter, we have been concerned in more than one instance to distinguish between two components of love in discussing the dynamics of the love relationship; namely, the difference in the demands of erotic love in relation to those of sublimated or romantic love. Each has been categorized and discussed in terms of specific characteristics and mutual influence. The suggestion has been that erotic love usually does not last and remains unsatisfied, creating a tendency for the disillusioned lover to move from one love object to the next in an endless series of attempts to re-find the underlying root, as it were, to his need to idealize each successive encounter of his desire. The question may arise whether there might be a third way, as it were; that is, whether there might be a third kind of love that, perhaps a combination of aspects of the two aforementioned, might spell a more optimistic picture of the viability of lasting love.

Mitchell (2002), in offering some thoughts on the idea of romantic love, sheds some light on this possibility in his discussion of the "degradation" of romance: how and why it happens. In the forward to *Can Love Last*, Margaret Black, his wife, reminds us that modern life, at all levels of the socio-economic scale, can be difficult, draining and confusing. Against such a dissatisfying reality, people seek the robustness and promise of a better experience in romance that holds out the possibility of falling in love and, with it, the promise of replacing heart-ache with love. Yet, because, as we have said, falling in love is so fueled by illusion, that, following initial consummations, it readily degrades into something else "much less captivating and much less enlivening." Mitchell's list includes such replacements as "a merely sober respect, a merely diversionary excursion into sexuality, a predictable [but uneventful] companionship, or, worse, hatred, guilt and self-pity" (p. 27).

As romance thrives upon mystery and a sense of excitement, we oscillate between a dialectic of loneness and connection with the object of our enchantment. Both seem frightening and risky. As Lacan says (Mitchell, 2002), "love is giving something you don't have to someone you don't know." Therein lies the rub; for such connection, founded as it is so upon fantasy and wish, can't help but be less than rational. Yet it seems we can't help but strive for the new and exciting. But we also want the safety and security of the familiar; of what we have known early on in family and home. While generally speaking, men are less dependent upon familiarity than women, nonetheless, the dependency longings they do harbor are not reinforced in a culture that too often insists upon male roles of self-made independence and autonomy. Meanwhile, though women are in principle no less adventurous than their male counterparts, nonetheless, the more traditional female role requirements of our culture often seem to compromise these more robust impulses.

The picture is complicated by the fact, stated many times before, that the alliance between passion and commitment is always tenuous and unstable at best. Historically, romantic love was seen as but a prelude to a more stable, lasting love. Yet with the expectations created by the sexual revolution, such cautionary wisdom was discarded for the search for unending pleasure and gratification in one's partner or partners. Women, too, were seen as needing and being entitled to these same gratifications as their male counterparts. Mitchell notes that although sexual equality between the sexes and the sense of entitlement to continuing sexual fulfillment regardless of the cost has been tempered somewhat with the advent of AIDS and the prevalence of other sexually transmitted diseases; yet "most of us still believe that our self is reflected and expressed in our sexuality, a belief that makes the pursuit of romance, within or outside long standing relationships, a popular life's work" (p. 42). Although it may be true that becoming accustomed to one another in a relationship has the collateral effect of dulling the romance, nonetheless, it may also be true that such "dulling" is not intrinsic to love, but might be better understood as a defense against the vulnerabilities opened up by the vicissitudes of romantic love already discussed.

Though Mitchell is somewhat critical of Freud's observation concerning love, on the whole, he seems to agree with him. We all have to negotiate the ambivalence of love and loving, and it takes an act of will to be proficient at it. Yet, it seems, we have little choice as desire and passion are not mere contrivances of will, and, often seemingly outside of our control are, nonetheless, so shaping and important to our lives that it is hard to imagine a life worth living without them. Yet, Mitchell reminds us, we need to remember that these important relationships occur in contexts that we construct. If a romantic commitment is to last, he counsels, then we need to guard against stasis and to dedicate ourselves to a process of discovery in the face of uncertainty. Yet in our steadfast commitment, we must guard against being so rigid as to pre-empt spontaneity; while the goal of spontaneity can not be so rigid as to preclude commitment. The mere resolution of sexual tension is not sufficient to guarantee the building of a relationship. There must also be a sense of commitment to a process of discovery in the relationship where each in the couple have a sense of fascination by the ways in which, individually and together, they generate a form of life, open-textured and resilient, that they can each count on and that is a never ending source of comfort and mystery. This, then, is Mitchell's recipe for a "third way", as it were, to sustain and maintain the spirit of love.

REFERENCES

Freud, S. (1910) Contributions to the psychology of love. A special type of choice of object made by men. *Collected Papers, IV,* 192–202.

———. (1912).Contributions to the psychology of love. The most prevalent form of degradation in erotic life. *Collected Papers, IV,* 203–216.

———. (1918) Contributions to the psychology of love. The taboo of virginity. *Collected Papers, IV:*217–235.

Mitchell, S.A. (2002) *Can Love Last? The Fate of Romance Over Time.* New York: W. W. Norton & Company.

Shuren, I. (1975) Perspectives on love: psychoanalytic considerations. *Issues in Ego Psychology, 1:*19–28.

Chapter Three

Sexuality

SEXUALITY

Sexuality is not love, but love includes sexuality. The idea of romantic love involves the idea of a perfect match in one's beloved. Such a partner will be not only wonderfully attractive, but be also perfectively sensitive to the needs and desires, as well as being the exclusive possession of, the lover. Catholic women, for example (Davis, 2002), will inform their lovers (when desiring to get married) that, once married, their breasts will belong to their lover exclusively, anytime and anywhere.

These sorts of idealizations are indispensable to the notion of romantic love and fuel the fantasy of wanting to be as close to such a love object as is physically possible; the wish, as it were, to actually incorporate the lover. We recognize such fantasies as being fueled by the consequence of the lover having projected part of his narcissistic libido, his ego ideal, onto the love object (especially in physical terms), and note that when this transfer of narcissistic libido is returned by the loved one, a state of bliss results in the body and "soul" of the lover. The idea is that by incorporating the other in this way, the yearning for completion in the arms of the beloved is realized (that is, the lover is reunited with his powerful narcissistic projection through union with his beloved), and his longings for union and merger are, for the time being, quelled. When this happens we might say, in a more clinical mode, that the tension between the ego and the ego-ideal has been markedly reduced.

This idea of merger through union in this sense has been observed by Steiner (2002). It was Kernberg (1995), however, who stated that such couples become, as it were, a subgroup distinct from the larger cultural group from whence they came because, once in love, they have little or no interest in anything outside of their love.

People making such narcissistic object choices, however, are bound to end up disappointed. Those who cling so anxiously to their partners often develop feelings of intense jealousy, envy and even hate. With the dwindling of sexual passion and the realization of difference between self and beloved (Fenchel, 1995), disillusionment in the fantasy of blissful oneness with the other begins to set in, the spell of enchantment is broken and stormy idealization is replaced by depression. It takes a well structured personality with well developed boundaries to be able to weather (and integrate) the ambivalences inherent in any relationship, and especially those built solely upon narcissistic projections. Bergmann (1998) remarks, that the possibility of loving an object non-narcissistically is a late, fragile and never complete acquisition for the child, while Freud's notion of mature love stressed the need for a blend of romantic passion with disenchanted realism.

In literature are often found rather cogent and insightful remarks about sexual infatuation and falling in love. Toni Morrison (2003) puts it this way:

> Do they still call it infatuation? That magic ax that chops away the world in one blow, leaving only the couple standing there trembling? Whatever they call it, it leaps over anything, takes the biggest chair, the largest slice, rules the ground wherever it walks, from a mansion to a swamp, and its selfishness is its beauty (p.61). Reprinted by permission of International Creative Management, Inc. Copyright 2003 by Toni Morrison.

In her book, *Love,* Morrison calls sex "the clown of love." She sees sexual love as an experimental and risky business fraught with disappointments. Because it is often so driven primarily by the physical, she sees it as too unstable to support a more long lasting and satisfying intimacy based, as it is, upon a less heady capacity for mutual give and take by each party in the relationship. Intimacy of this sort requires the capacity to tolerate separateness as well as unity, something at odds with the narcissistic fantasy of merger and physical oneness. Love rooted so essentially in the physical, she says, is not intelligent love. Like a showpiece, it is selfish and romantic, cut off from the real world (almost in opposition to it). In following only its own dictates, it is narcissistic, exhibitionistic and, often, tragic because, in the end, for all its vaunted exclusiveness and separateness from the real world, it is the real world, she says, that, ultimately, wins. Other literary examples of the seeming, inherently frustrated and tragic trajectory of romantic, sexual love can be found in Abelard and Eloise, Romeo and Juliet, Othello.

But must all sexual and romantic encounters end in tragedy? Of course not; but whether it does or does not depends completely upon the persons so involved as well as the circumstances of their involvement. If we are to understand the possibility of successful and gratifying love, however, we need first to understand (and decipher) the complex motivations and compulsions that often, together, tend to frustrate its fully realized expression.

Silverman (2001) informs us about the complex relationship between erotic desire and attachment, the latter constituting a system of particular importance since it regulates affect that is primary in coordinating and grounding one's sense of "rootedness" and "aliveness" in one's sense of self. If attachment is fragile, a sense of depression, shame and guilt can ensue, potentially ruining a love relationship by replacing the love by a malignant aggression. Aggression, then, is an important factor potentially derailing love. Indeed, as we move ahead in our exploration of the conditions of the possibility of mature love, it will be important to keep in mind that with hate (an earlier and more primitive emotion than the mature love we seek to understand), always, as it were, lurking in the background, ambivalence rather than non-ambivalence is much more likely to be the rule in any love relationship; making it important always to consider the sources and effects of ambivalence in understanding the complexities of the dynamics of mature love. True enough. However, we need first to address the nature of primitive, raw sexuality before we discuss the viability of mature love in a state of ambivalence.

When speaking of eroticism (Fenchel, 2000), it is important first to discuss the various implications to the concept of libido derived from its various usages in Freud. In general, we might say, libido is an impelling drive or force that seeks satisfaction in intense physical pleasure that tends to satisfy a variety of needs. Yet Freud speaks of it in at least three ways: first as a non-specific energy expressed as underlying any connection or cathexsis of any sort; secondly, more specifically, as one of the drives composing his dual drive theory; and, thirdly, more specifically still, as the imminent force propelling psychosexual development through the stages of oral, anal and, finally, phallic/genital organization. To make matters even less clear, earlier, before the completion of the dual drive model, Freud referred to "sexual interest and stimulation" in a variety of behavioral and mental representations in relation to one another. Affection, attachment to persons and lust all indicated the underlying unity of libidinal drives, while the psychosexual stages invested certain body parts with pleasure depending on maturation and education. We need to distinguish, then, between 'libido' in general and in terms of the dual drive theory from psycho-sexual stages of development and pure erotic sexuality.

Libido describes the aim of a drive, namely fusion in contrast to the aim of the aggressive drive which seeks separation. But to speak of libido in this theoretical sense (as the abstraction of a drive to fusion) does not do justice to the force we mean to capture in speaking of libido in connection with the quality of pure "lust" associated with sexuality when we speak of 'sex' in its more concrete or unadulterated form. When we discuss sexuality as a theoretical matter, we are, indeed, addressing the outcome of psychosexual development focused, as it is, upon genital gratification. But when we speak of sex in its concrete sense, we are speaking of a force not abstract or theoretical, but rather as something that drives coitus, something both urgent and with a force, as it were, of a "hurricane."

In Talmudic writings, this force was acknowledged as a strong biological imperative in men especially, while women were described as being more inhibited. Perhaps these writings suggest the difference that, whereas in men the drive to sex is experienced as a powerful centrifugal force as it were, in woman it is known more only as a centripetal counterpart. In any event, these biologically "given" and omnipresent sexual thoughts and temptations in men, though considered normal, nonetheless, were considered in need of regulation. Nor was it thought that having these urges had anything to do with one's character or social status (see, for example, King David). However, Telushkin (1994) suggests that, to the contrary, it may have been thought that the greater the social status of the man, the greater his evil inclinations. In any case, while marriage was considered the most appropriate outlet to regulate this drive, rape, incest and adultery were admitted so long as they were perpetrated by the man far away from his home and under disguise. More often, though, sexuality was regulated as part of social and religious custom. One such custom allowed that laborers and donkey drivers could have sex twice a week while camel drivers could only engage in such practices once a month, with sailors being allowed such delights only once every six months.

Because of the importance of maintaining a family structure to society, sexual union between a man and a woman was considered an aspect of marriage that should not admit of external compromise. Indeed, adultery was considered a betrayal not only against one's spouse, but also as against God. However, the woman's marital status was decisive in considering the question of adultery. By definition, it was only possible for a married woman to be a party to adultery. If she were single, and therefore available for marriage, she could never be accused of adultery.

In our present society, sex is considered a narcissistic entitlement to be enjoyed starting in one's teens. Moreover, were it not for the fear of contracting a sexually transmitted disease (and especially the fear of contracting AIDS), it seems doubtful whether there would continue to be such an emphasis on sex education and the use of condoms as prevails in the current climate of contagion. Indeed, some researchers point out that in spite of such efforts and in spite of the attempts to inculcate the message of moral abstinence, sexual behavior not only has not decreased, but, overall has increased and especially among adolescents where it is viewed both as a necessary rite of passage and as a status symbol.

Kardiner (1954), an anthropologist, remarked that the ideas of sexual taboos began because it was necessary to protect prepubescent girls, with a capacity to be impregnated, from the sexual excesses of older males. Yet he points out that the attempt to control the sexuality of both sexes during childhood cannot exclude arousal patterns that are largely the result of accident or imagination. In any case, the cost of too rigid control of sexuality in the name of social stability, he points out, often leads to inhibition of mature sexual functioning in adult life, a price, he suggests, we may no longer need to pay:

> Sex morality, with many of its implementations, once served the ends of social survival. This is no longer the case. Our survival now depends on very different contingencies (p.159).

According to Ruth Stein (1998), we need to reconfigure our understanding of sexuality away from the way it is prefigured by the controlling metaphor of drive and object relations. She speaks of it as a distinctly poignant, enveloping experience of a unique pleasure composed of both sensory and affective currents, aroused through the direct stimulation of the skin. The intense yield of pleasure arising from such stimulation allows gratification of a variety of needs and wishes, the most central being to reinforce a sense of self-identity. Relational theorists also acknowledge the transformative qualities of this urge, the juice that potentates and embellishes all experience.

An example of a woman's experience of eroticism and thralldom, perhaps suggesting the above, is illustrated by D. H. Lawrence's, (1982), *Lady Chatterley's Lover*.

As Lady Chatterley consummated her orgiastic sexual experience with her lover, she becomes aware of how rewarding it was for her in many different ways. She speaks of tender love towards an unknown man and submitting to his potent penis. As the latter is withdrawn "and left her body," she experienced a sense of deep loss and tried to put it back. She could not bear separating from it.

Eroticism is the best kept secret during our development. Parents don't talk about it. It is the symbol of an enigma and hidden truth. It cannot be captured completely in words, nor is it within the purview of logical thought. It inspires one to transgress taboos, yet is akin to the sacred and the holy, different and set apart. Word derivation from back in time attests to its complexity and enigmatic meaning. For example, in Hebrew the etymological root for eroticism is to be found both in the word 'holiness' and 'prostitute,' both having in common the etymological derivation from the idea of being "set apart" and "chosen." The anthropologist, Bataille (1957), points out that both religion and sexuality express the deepest longing to return to a primordial unity in which all difference is merged into an undifferentiated continuity allowing, through the loss of all vestiges of psychic individuality, an escape from loneliness. Eroticism in this sense is the desire to give oneself up and to live the limits of both the possible and the impossible with ever increasing intensity. In this sense, both religion and sexuality can be said to undermine, by breaking down and dissolving, order, and, in so doing, tend to the creation of disorder born, on the one hand, out of the need for self-transcendence and, on the other hand, out of the anguished need for the unattainable object of erotic merger (Fenchel, 1998).

Eroticism also contains elements of sadism as discussed and explored in the work of both Kernberg (1992) and Stoller (1979). There occurs an exploitation of the object for the purpose of pleasure. Hostility, serving to convert childhood trauma into adult triumph, is said to be central to the feeling of sexual excitement not only in perverse sexuality, but in its non-perverse forms as well. Such excitement involves the rapid oscillations of pain/pleasure, relief/trauma, success/failure and danger/safety. Thus erotic sexuality is invigorating and even violent. Passionate love, therefore, has the power for both good and evil. It can both exploit the beloved's need for illusions, while providing a sense of transcending mere mundane reality for a higher truth. It involves the attempt to bring unity and harmony to unconscious wishes and fantasies and so is, in part, totally embracing of the irrational. Yet because male sexuality is so much more straight forward than female sexuality, important differences between the sexes in terms of difference in the nature of the actual somatic experience of such by men and women, can not be entirely left out of the realm of plausible speculation.

REFERENCES

Bataille, G. (1957) *Eroticism: Death and Sexuality. Tran. M. Daelwood.* San Francisco: City Light Books.

Bergman, M. (1998) Love and intimacy. *Issues in Psychoanalytic Psychology, 20:*97–112.

Davis, R. (2002) Love escapes extinction. *Conference of the British Psychoanalytical Society, 2002.*

Fenchel, G. (1995) The narcissism of minor differences. Love and hate in intimate relationships. *Issues in Psychoanalytic Psychology, 17:*84–93.

———. (1998) Exquisite intimacy—dangerous love. *Issues in Psychoanalytic Psychology, 20:*17–27.

———. (2000) Eroticism and the conventional. *Journal of the American Academy of Psychoanalysis, 28:*163–173.

Fromm, E. (1956) *The Art of Loving.* New York: Harper & Rowe.

Kardiner, A. (1954) *Sex and Morality.* New York: Bobbs-Merill

Kernberg, O. (1992) *Aggression in Personality Disorders and Perversions.* New Haven: Yale University Press.

———. (1995) *Love Relations.* New Haven: Yale University Press.

Lawrence, D. H. Lady Chatterley's Lover. In: *Love: A Celebration of Art & Literature,* (ed.) Jahn Lahr and Lena Tabori, p. 146. New York: Stewart, Tabori & Chaing Publishers, 1982.

Morrison, T. (2003) *Love.* New York: Alfred Knopf.

Silverman, D. (2001) Sexuality and attachment: a passionate relationship or a marriage of convenience? *Psychoanalytic Quarterly, 52:*325–358.

Stein, R. (1998) The poignant, the excessive and the enigmatic in sexuality. *International Journal of Psycho-Analysis, 79:*253–268.

Steiner, R. (2002) Freud on love: an historical overview. *Conference of the British Psychoanalytic Society.* 2002.

Stoller, J. (1979) *Sexual Excitement. The Dynamics of Erotic Life.* New York: Pantheon Books.

Telushkin, J. (1994) *Jewish Wisdom.* New York: William Morrow.

Chapter Four

Intimacy

THE MADNESS OF INTIMACY

The word 'intimacy' denotes the revelation of one's most innermost thoughts and feelings; perhaps, even, the unveiling of secrets. This state can be experienced with oneself as well as with another. As it is libidinal, it functions as a connection between oneself and another. Although sometimes used as a euphemism for sexual intercourse, it is different in being characterized primarily in terms of non-sexual aims. It is true, however, that a sensual and tactile intimacy may be established in sexual expression, but this sense of intimacy is more about immediate gratification derived from the sense of interpenetration of selves that results primarily from the flush of bodily contact. In contrast, the sense of aim-inhibited intimacy primarily in question here, is more a matter of symbolic contact and suggests a later developmental achievement in which there is a coherent, independent self capable of object constancy (hence, capable of mature dependency upon an object recognized, at least in part, as separate from self).

In everyday interactions, relating occurs on many different levels. What we say consciously to each other, for example, may not have the same meaning or intent as it does on unconscious levels. Indeed, conscious words and behavior often carry unconscious transferential meaning coloring our interactions giving them meanings we do not intent or have conscious control over. The nature of the libidinal unconscious has been explored by Bergmann (1988) and Langs (1986) who state that more than we know, many decisions are made on an unconscious level the content of which is not revealed in our manifest communications to one another. For example, a wife who consistently tries to discredit her husband's competency may actually, at an unconscious level, be playing out her jealousy and envy towards her husband's ex-wife. Loewald (1949), too, echoes the fact that ordinary, everyday perception and interaction among persons is constituted on many different levels, many of which are unconscious. A corollary to this is the fact that the more self aware we are (that is, the more the unconscious is integrated with and known by the conscious mind), the broader the conscious range of response levels to perception. The mature ego, integrated in this way, incorporates the energy from earlier dynamic states of being, and is enlivened by the unimpeded flow of such previously damned up sources of energy hitherto lost by the repression of its infantile sources. When the Ego is not sufficiently developed in this way and one is more than less in the dark about oneself, integration is deficient and behavior is often erratic and inchoate because the self is not sufficiently at one, or in harmony, with its unconscious derivatives, Joseph (1987).

To achieve intimacy, couples have to overcome many obstacles including, to name a few, differences in style, differences in family background, morality and the many, unspoken primitive fears each feels in relation to the other. As Freud pointed out, though, conflict often erupts over seemingly the most "minor" of differences. For example, a former patient of mine once recounted to me that he had divorced his wife because he could not tolerate her rolling up the toilet paper the way she did. Green (1966) labeled the dynamics surrounding such differences as a sort of "private madness."

Of course, the fact that situations of intimacy can provoke such "madness" attests to the power unconscious fears and wishes have upon conscious affect. Moreover, because the conscious mind is always more or less in a battle with the regressive activation of unconscious derivatives from one's infantile life and objects, the conscious aims of maturity are often conflicted by these unconscious aims and wishes, creating behaviors, sometimes bizarre or self defeating, reflecting accommodations to these conflicts called 'compromise formations.' One such regressive pull is caused by the infantile wish for, and narcissistic gratification in, the fantasy of return and union with the symbiotic mother. As pointed out in chapter two above, such a wish, if not integrated, can wreak havoc in one's love life! Yet clinical observations show that many patients suffer from conflicts caused by a myriad of narcissistic slights and hurts experienced each day that resonate with the deep need for restitution and repair of the many and sometimes lasting narcissistic wounds suffered early in life and often in relation to the mother.

With so much need for healing, is it no wonder that it is the attribution of healing qualities in the lover that makes the lover lovable and that fosters the conditions for intimate revelation and sharing? Yet intimacy, like love, is not necessarily an enduring state. It remains alive just so long as the relationship is suffused with the warm glow of reflected, mutual adoration and seeming unconditional acceptance. While in such states, we feel neither defensive, jealous, envious or hateful, but, rather, trusting, open and loving. Thus, in most instances, it is true to say that intimacy and love are intertwined and often go hand in hand with an abiding sense of harmony and transcendence quite unique from the ordinary self states experienced in the common day to day routine of ordinary living.

Except in perversions, to experience intimacy is a sign that love has won out over hate. Yet if wishes for total attention or unlimited, unconditional love become too paramount in the relationship, are demanded but not fulfilled, angry and defensive operations are likely to take place fouling the climate for intimacy and stopping (or inhibiting) the flow of good feeling. According to Sands (1985), a possible defense to such a narcissistic blow, might be the removal of oneself from such an involvement by retreating to an inner emotional construct of romantic nostalgia wherein is preserved the idealized but lost object and sense of self. The trauma caused by the anticipated disappointment and loss of such objects can often trigger regressive maneuvers of mind causing one to fall back on more primitive modes of relating. In such narcissistic regressions grandiose and deflated self images are often in precarious balance and the reactivated, primitive, sadistic impulses once bound by the more complex and differentiated ego, become diffuse and in need of modulation and re-metabolization.

Romantic intimacy can also be studied by reviewing the way couples have been depicted by the great poets of romantic literature. The European romantic movement was especially interested in, and seemed to be attracted to, reflecting the extremes of physical passions, the supernatural, the melancholic and the more cruel aspects of love. It emphasized imagination and emotion over reason and intellect. Famous English exemplars of this movement were Shelley, Byron, Keats while in Germany principle proponents include Schiller, Novalis and Goethe. According to the tenants of this romanticism, the here and now of appearance belies greater organic forces underlying and infusing the surface of things as, for example, one experiences in a moment of sublime transcendence the sense of the divine, the god head, as it were, that inspires recognition of a deeper sense of self in identification with the underlying power of nature. Thus, there is the quest, underlying much of romantic idealization, for sublime union with a power greater than, though imminent in, the realm of mere mundane circumstance. Likewise, by surrendering self and ego to another, one is impelled by the fantasy of being magically transformed, as it were, by this encounter into a completely different psychic reality, a transcendent reality of unity and relatedness in the form of "a couple" (the same fantasy, perhaps, driving the fairy tale wish that at the moment of giving over to and kissing the frog, the plain little girl will suddenly be transformed into a princess and the frog into a magical prince).

"The couple," arises, then, as a sort of "created third" constructed out of the unconscious expectations each has of the consequences of their commingling. The fantasy driving the construct of the "created third" in this sense may facilitate a greater degree of attunement of each to the other and, in the process of coupling, promote the evolution of a specialization of roles between each in relation to each other allowing modifications of internal self and object representations. If marital conflicts intrude upon this system in a recurring fashion, the result may lead to a polarization within the relationship in which the partners experience one another as irreconcilable opposites. On the other hand, when properly attuned to each other, a sense of intimacy suffuses the relationship and each is possessed of a sense of well being and satisfaction. When not so properly attuned, however, intimacy is no longer felt possible and the loss is met with a certain anxiety and, fearing its lack, the couple may resort to fighting in order to fill up the gap of felt, lost connection. Fighting, at least, in offering involvement and engagement, however destructive, is better than the feared emptiness of disinterest and unconnectedness.

While some surrender to the other is involved in intimacy as a normal regression in the service of the ego, fighting and bickering may also become a stable way of life. Marriages of more pathologically regressed individuals such as with borderline personalities and manic depressive individuals, involve dynamics based upon more primitive internal fantasies that are expressed by manifest magical and mystical expectations (Fenchel, 1998). In such couples, partners often represent magical objects needed to fulfill these primitive, psychic needs. Paramount among these expectations includes the need for total gratification, instant intimacy and fusion. While much is sacrificed and given up, even more is expected in return. When partners to such fused expectations experience the other as separate, they become frustrated, angry and depressed. With aggression turned against the self and the partner, intimacy tends to be replaced by sado-masochism.

Although coupling for the most part is beneficial both psychologically and physiologically, nonetheless, it behooves each of us so desiring such union to bear in mind the proviso "at your own risk: potentially dangerous to your health!" When, for example, roles within an intimate relationship differ widely from the personalities projected outside the relationship, serious problems may occur (Willi, 1982). Such intensive relationships over a period of time may result in personality changes in both partners. For each to live with the other peacefully something from each may have to be given up reducing options and freedom. The idea of such "partial renunciation" by partners in a couple has been illustrated extensively by Kernberg (1976). Willi (1982) poses the question of what the optimal degree of fusion and separateness might be for a couple in order to allow for emotional health and satisfactory relatedness, and answers by saying: "It is in the middle range between these two extremes that allows for normal function" (p.18).

Much of the confusion about marriage results from the predisposition to thinking it is a stable state within which each of the partner's sense of self-esteem will ever be secure, protected and defended against the external world. But the decision to couple and the reality of such relatedness involves, inherently, fundamental constraints upon the making of basic choices that are necessary in fostering a firm sense of identity. Magical solutions to such frustrations, not unlike those states observed in mystical religiosity (Fenchel, 1998), often ensue and there sets in a distancing from reality oriented relating. The conflict soon becomes one of intimacy versus independence. Kernberg (1976) succinctly describes this situation in his account of how the mutual interactions of a couple tend to vacillate between, on the one hand, renouncements for the sake of the partner in order, in fantasy, to secure, on the other hand, a greater enrichment arising out of the sense of refinding oneself in the recognition of the other. As mentioned above, however, such regressive, fusion driven fantasies are often destructive to the desire of close intimacy (even though fueled by such desire), as they tend to reactivate primitive dynamics associated with the situation of undifferentiated fusion in symbiosis. In less pathological coupling, the sense of separateness experienced by one partnered with the other is tolerable as only a momentary disillusionment, and is compensated by the realization that the partner's individuality can also bring enrichment to the self by broadening one's own freedom and individuality in the context of intimacy; a felt recognition that separateness is not necessarily in opposition to loving.

Willi (1982) applies a psychoanalytic typology in understanding these themes we have been discussing in our analysis of the dynamics of couples and coupling. For example, in couples defined by more narcissistic needs, conflict is oriented around the issue of how much of reality is to be sacrificed in the process of satisfying the fantasy need to be perfectly mirrored by the other. In such relating "the oral" gets expressed and the central issue becomes the question of how much one's partner can approximate, in taking care of oneself, the unconditional love and nurture of an unselfish mother. "Oral coupling" is also sometimes fueled by the fantasy of self-healing. Conflict arises when the partner ceases to fulfill the needed fantasy and satisfaction can no longer be obtained. At that point the illusion of a healed oneness in and through the other turns into disillusionment and the "good" mother is turned into the "bad" mother.

On the other hand, under the forces of regression arising out of the desire to possess the partner completely, sadomasochistic dynamics may develop reactivating the expression of "anal" conflicts over power and control in the context of possession. In this, the most frequent form of marital conflict, the relationship becomes transformed into a sort of master-slave dynamic where the "active" partner demands autonomy, leadership and control while the more "passive" partner accepts the role of submission and dependence in order to defend against what are usually the same abandonment fears that underlie, however unconsciously, the stance of the seemingly more powerful partner. (Interestingly, the turning point in such conflict within the anal regressed couple usually occurs when the repressed fears of the active, more dominant partner in the couple become conscious. At that point, anxiety becomes overwhelming and the couple usually breaks down.)

Finally, for partners coexisting in the context of more oedipal level organization and development, the woman may be under sway to repress her more male characteristics while the man may be similarly so predisposed to repress his feminine identifications or traits. Every couple must negotiate these themes and find a solution acceptable to both partners.

Failure to master such conflicts usually bespeaks greater problems in integrating much deeper conflicts with much more pronounced and destabilizing effects reactivated from the childhood of each partner in the context of the regressive pull inherent in the coupling process. For example, in the narcissistic relationship where union is fueled by the wish for total oneness, the partner exists only as a fantasized object without any separate reality or autonomy outside of the fantasy. Such individuals are often opposed to marriage and if pressured into one may prefer to remain childless. In all of this, the choice and success of the partnership is usually dependent upon how much idealization can be sustained by each in the context of the couple. Even the maximal sense of intimacy may be insufficient to sustain marriages if fault lines develop that are too great for the couple to master.

To conclude this chapter, and in summary, we might say that the selection of partners to a couple depends upon how much sense of confirmation and self-affirmation a prospective partner is seen in fantasy to be able to give in reflecting recognition of, and reinforcement to, one's need to be reunited with one's own projected idealized self-image (ego ideal). Such choices appear to set in motion a dynamic process of adaptation by each partner in the relationship wherein certain specific needs, fears and ideals, assume unusual predominance, while other aspects of these same individuals remain more or less unaffected by their coupling. Yet, the fantasy underlying the fascination that fuels the intensity of mutual attraction can only take place in the context of frustration and absence in the real world of precisely that need for self-completion and self-transcendent oneness that is found by each to be lacking without the other. Only by its absence, then, does the urge for completeness in and through someone other make itself known as a urgent need, where the feeling is that one will be "re-found," as it were, and so re-united, in the gaze of the desired other with something that is otherwise seemingly lost and forever out of reach.

REFERENCES

Bergmann, M. (1988) Freud's three theories of love in the light of later developments. *Journal of the American Psychoanalytic Association, 36:*653–672.

Fenchel, G. (1998) Exquisite intimacy-dangerous love: a study of Jewish mysticism. *Issues in Psychoanalytic Psychology, 20:*17–28.

Green, A. (1986) *On Private Madness.* New York: International Universities Press.

Joseph, E. (1987) The consciousness of being conscious. *Journal of the American Psychoanalytic Association, 35:*5–22.

Kernberg, O. (1976) *Object Relations Theory and Clinical Psychoanalysis.* New York: Aronson.

———. (1977) Boundaries and structures in love relations. *Journal of the American Psychoanalytic Association, 25:*81–114.

Langs, R. (1986) Clinical issues arising from a new model of the mind. *Contemporary Psychoanalysis, 22:*418–444.

Loewald, H. (1949) Ego and reality. In: *Papers on Psycho-Analysis,* p. 3–20. New Haven: Yale University Press.

Sands,S. (1985) Narcissism as a defense against object loss: Stendhal and Proust. *Psychoanalytic Review, 72:*105–127.

Willi, J. (1982) *Couples in Collusion.* New York: Aronson.

Chapter Five

Development of Love

DEVELOPMENTAL ASPECTS OF LOVE

Freud's theory of psychosexual development (1910) included the idea that love in life begins from the very beginning with the love between infant and caretaking mother and, later, is further elaborated in its transference from the mother to the father. It was Freud's idea that these early love experiences form a template, as it were, for all future love relationships in the life of the maturing individual. When the physical care of the infant, that necessarily involves bodily contact of the skin, is administered with loving affect, the infant feels trusting and taken care of. Without such accompanying affect by the caretaker, however, the infant becomes anxious and ambivalent. The impact of the maternal environment and the love experienced in these early times forever thereafter sets in motion, as the little boy grows older, a search to refind the lost bliss of this now idealized early stage of life. Thus, the love objects for adult men, in one way or the other (with some interesting complications in homosexual love), forever thereafter, take on the form symbolic of the mother.

Women develop somewhat differently. According to Freud, women begin, of course, by loving the mother but, becoming aware of their anatomical difference from boys, become ambivalent towards her who, they feel, is responsible for their lacking a penis. This ushers into place a sort of "tom boy phase' where the little girl acts out a phallic presence that, ultimately unsustainable, gives way to interest in the father and the wish to possess his penis in the form of having his "penis baby." Development may be interfered with if there is too much penis envy. In either case however, in order to enjoy non-conflicted sexual love in a mature state, both boys and girls have to master, by overcoming, the incestuous "undertones" born of their infantile romance with the parent of the opposite sex.

Because women, unlike men, must change their object of infantile passion from the mother, their first love object, to the father, Freud (1931) says female development is more fraught with possibility to go wrong than is the case of male development where such a change of original love object does not have to occur. Thus, the realization of satisfactory mature loving is often more difficult for women than for men. There are many women, for example, who are arrested at the pre-oedipal phase of psychosexual development owing, particularly, to their tie to the mother and, correspondingly, have difficulty negotiating the switch of libidinal interest to the father. This makes sense given the complexity of their requisite developmental achievement and suggests that the pre-oedipal phase of development may play a more significant role in understanding the vicissitudes of loving for women than it does for men.

Understanding this in terms of the relevant related erogenous zone of psychosexual development, suggests that the important phallic infantile psychosexual response to the mother, the first love object for both boys and girls, is similar for both boys and girls. Indeed, for just as the boy has his penis with which to masturbate so too initially, in what Freud described as a female phallic phase, the little girl masturbates with her clitoris. During this period, according to Freud, vaginal sensations are non-existent in the little girl. What then, one might ask, triggers the need in the little girl to switch objects and discover the psychosexual aspects of the vagina? Freud believes that girls feel very ambivalent about their mother since, in fantasy, they imagine her to be castrated and, therefore, lacking a certain presence, fullness or completion and, therefore, in some sense being wanting or "inferior." Finding herself also to be lacking or "castrated" and, in this sense, like the mother, the little girl comes to resent the mother for this deficiency and of being like her. She, too, feels inferior and, struggling against these feelings, may rebel and develop a masculine complex in defense against her penis envy. Such is the situation in the stormy pre-oedipal phase of female psychosexual development according to Freud. (Later, of course, as mentioned above, with the transition to the Oedipus complex, she discovers the fantasy of having what she lacks in having the father's phallus in the form of having his "penis baby.") A consequence of her ambivalence toward the mother in this pre-oedipal phase, however, is the generation in her of fantasies of a dangerous mother. In one such, for example, the little girl's projected rage at the mother may be experienced by her as the fantasy of a retaliating, sadistic, cannibalistic, devouring mother. Thus Freud observes:

> Perhaps the real fact is that the attachment to the mother must inevitably perish just because it is the first and most intense, similarly to what we so often find in

the first marriages of young women , entered into when they were most passionately in love. In both cases the love relation probably comes to grief by reason of the inevitable disappointments and an accumulation of occasions for aggression. As a rule the second marriages turn out much better (p.262).

Even though Freud was convinced of his psychological observations, he cautiously added that it was not possible with any degree of certainty to distinguish the contribution of genetics or biology on the one hand and, on the other hand, of the effects of fantasy in light of accident of environmental factors and their impact on an impressionable and malleable psyche.

He then turns to observations on how choices of partners come about. In this, and in light of persisting traces of oedipal conflict in men, he noted the tendency in men to be less conflicted sexually with women who, in the unconscious, were distinguishable from the mother. Since the mother in most men is retained in an idealized relation, Freud noticed that such men were better able to find sexual release with a woman degraded and so differentiated from the mother in this respect and, therefore, allowing less inhibited sexual experience. If she were already in relation to another man, and for the same oedipal reasons as before, this would make her more attractive, even if potentially more conflicted: a forbidden fruit as it were.

A virtuous and respectable woman never possesses the charm to exalt her to an object of love; this attraction is exercised only by one who is more or less sexually discredited, whose fidelity and loyalty admit of some doubt (p.194).

Freud was addressing here sexual passion which has been augmented by jealousy and rivalry.

In less conflicted love, although there may be loyalty and fidelity, nonetheless without the dimension of forbidden fruit, as it were, the love is less likely to be experienced with the same degree of passion as the love of the forbidden love of one's sexual rival. The inflamed lover has the fantasy of rescuing the women from an inferior or, more likely, tyrannical possessor and, in so doing, the lover in the fantasy of rescuing his forbidden beloved is actually rescuing his own otherwise doomed and frustrated love. Moreover, under the influence of an oedipal repetition, the pattern is repeated over and over again as the satisfaction longed for is, in spite of all, never found in any surrogate.

In his discussion of psychical impotence (1912), he advised that both affection and sensuality need to combine. This, of course, is exactly what does not happen in the example above, for by chasing after the unattainable surrogate, the lover is too close to his forbidden oedipal object to be able to allow both affection and sexual pleasure to be combined. He retains affection for the idealized but not sexual object, while experiencing uninhibited, sexual

lust for the degraded split-off alternative. Yet when love and affection are separate, the love relationship remains merely capricious, easily upset and typically, without affection, lacking in tenderness: "Where such men love, they
have no desire and, where they desire they cannot love" (p.207). Another way
of putting it: such love degrades the sexual object while reserving for the incestuous object all the idealization meant normally for the sexual object.

> It has an ugly sound and a paradoxical as well, but nevertheless it must be said
> that whoever is to be really free and happy in love must have overcome his def-
> erence for women and come to terms with the idea of incest with mother or sis-
> ter (p.211)

Freud remarks with a certain resigned pessimism that erotic instincts are
hard to mold in a fashion allowing easy and absolute gratification. Indeed,
because love occurs in relation to organs often conflated in the unconscious
with those of excrement, civilization and its inevitable reaction formations
are often at odds with animal need and its lusty aims. Bergmann (1998) wonders, in such a framework where the word intimacy is never even mentioned,
whether Freud had any genuine respect whatsoever for the phenomenon of
the need of human beings for intimacy.

In 2002, The British Psychoanalytical Society sponsored a symposium on
Love. Ricardo Steiner informs us that the word "love" is expressed in relation
to a great many and diverse kinds of emotional relationships, but he wonders
whether there really exists what some have extolled as "true love." The boy
develops a sexual tie with the mother and ego identification with the father.
In puberty preparation has been made to re-find the sexual object outside the
body, that is, the mother's breast. This is the prototype of all love. Yet, because the desire is so impelling and immoderate, aggression is inherent to the
sense of driven-ness.

Recalling the archaic ambivalence between the "good" and "bad" breast,
hate is always present on the scene of recovering the externalized breast in the
surrogate or substitute love object. The loss of the original breast is never
completely forgotten. Yet its reactivation reactivates with it the enormous ambivalence (see also M. Klein) of the original situation where hate prevailed
over contrary narcissistic trends. Because the primitive origin of the first attachment is retained even in more established trends of narcissistic libido, the
primitive tends to be an important feature or trend retained in all mature love
relationships as well.

The precarious nature of the drives can lead to fusion and diffusion depending upon the vicissitudes of super-ego development and maturation. The
more undeveloped and unintegrated the super-ego, the more harsh it is in its
tendencies and corresponding projections resulting in the activation of more

diffuse and primitive aggression in response to the felt persecutory projection. The effect of our destructive drives leads to increased guilt, conflict and resulting unhappiness. Yet even in the midst of such destructive fury, there exist a high degree of narcissistic gratification by the activation of the primitive ego's fantasy of omnipotence.

Steiner agrees with Freud that man has not lost his primitive nature and, therefore, there is built into the human condition an inescapable dimension of mutual hostility among human beings. On this view, the possibility of loving an object in the context of a relationship is a late, fragile and never complete acquisition for the adult rooted, as he is, in the conflicts of childhood. Freud's notion of mature love, as remarked earlier, was a blend of romantic passion and disenchanted realism.

Andre Green (2002) mentions the sense of liberation experienced in these fragile love relationships as creating, in the fantasy of union, a mystical "third" entity constituted, as it is, by the effects of over-idealization. Not only does such an idealized sense of physical union appeal to the senses, but it also heightens sensitivity. Such a lover wants to be as close to the love object as possible and to protect it from all possible harm as an expression of its utterly unique and irreplaceable nature. While such devotion admits of all self-sacrifice, ironically, however, the partner may not be in a state of symmetrical reciprocation of such devotion as feelings of jealousy may intrude. Because of the latter, the love is precarious, unsure, carrying with it the possibility of betrayal. (There is skepticism, perhaps, whether one deserves to be loved in what might seem an overly exaggerated devotion on the part of the seeking lover.) Yet, the need to be in permanent non-verbal communication with the other, as well as limited tolerance for any degree of separation, attests to the strength of the fantasy of re-finding the lost love object of childhood. Love and hatred, then, are inextricable because love and sexuality include these antagonistic aspects of idealization and narcissistic wound in the context of the dialectic between the "good" and the "bad" breast.

> They form a basic unity having to do with destruction and hate. The essence of love is narcissistic and grows from its unsatisfied nature. It is fundamentally the same as infantile love and fundamentally different from it (p.12).

Rosemary Davis (2002) extends and confirms this line of discussion. Because of its origin early on in the psychic development of the child, the mother's breast, as we have already noticed, is said to involve both narcissistic gratification through sucking and to activate sadistic impulses as well. Eros and Thanatos are intertwined, as it were, and the proportion of each in relation to the other will determine whether attachments are primarily libidinal and of an enduring nature, or, on the other hand, are primarily aggressive and, therefore, more fleeting (nasty, brutish and short), as, for example, when the sexual expression of such activates dynamics governed by jealousy and hate. Moreover, for a love relationship to be viable, the partners need to be somewhat symmetrical in their libidinal constitutions or the result is likely to end in "unrequited love," lamented by the poets since the Middle Ages as the situation where one partner pines for an attachment the other cannot reciprocate. Nor does a narcissistically motivated basis for partner selection, however exciting and exhilarating initially, necessarily bode well for longevity of the relationship. As noted, in such circumstances, as soon as the narcissistic bubble is burst by dissension, when serious disputes disrupt the illusion of oneness, love is abruptly withdrawn and de-idealization may unleash destructive aggression to ward off ensuing abandonment anxiety.

We have been recounting the pitfalls of love constituted in terms of primitive organization. The upshot seems to suggest that love is not likely to succeed unless more primitive stages of libidinal and aggressive trends are integrated by a psychic organization allowing of some degree of object constancy. However, where such achievement is fragile and vulnerable to diffusion under the pressure of coupling, where infatuation yields to primitive desire for merger, love can all too easily turn into its opposite. Successful relationships seem to depend, then, not only upon there being a strong cathexis connecting the pair, but also upon there being an abiding capacity by each for empathy for the other as well as a capacity by each to forego some degree of narcissistic gratification. A tall order to say the least!

Theodore Reik (1949), a student of Freud's, sought to revise libido theory. In doing so, he rejects the implication of psychosexual derivatives to the dynamics of loving and, instead, posits the idea that love is a process by which two people with some degree of infatuation with one another, nonetheless, are impelled as much by spiritual aims as not. Such love is far from the primitive thing we have been discussing to date; rather it expresses the quality of culture and civilization that Freud spoke of as only being possible in later life. Reik finds satisfaction in Freud's remark that we really know very little of love, but does not analyze love in the same way as Freud. Freud, as we know, sees sex as originating in the biological realm of instinct and reduction of tension created by instinct, while love, a late and higher achievement, is governed by the wish for psychic happiness. Thus, on Reik's reading of Freud, whereas sex seeks release of tension created by instinct or drive, love seeks psychic happiness:

> Sex can be casual about its object, love is always a personal relationship. It is possible to possess another person in sex but not in love. In love you can only belong to another person. You can force another person into sex but not love (p.19).

Reik takes the stance of what might be called a post-Freudian, ego psychological orientation in his discussions of love. Turning away from emphasis upon instincts and biological drives, Reik observes that falling in love has to do more with dissatisfaction in ourselves. Where we fall short, we seek in another the missing ego-ideal for ourselves. However, he is careful not to leave out the fact that the dynamics of seeking such a displaced ego ideal include the possibility of awakening jealousy, envy and hate. Successful love, then, must always involve, to some degree, a reaction formation against these aggressive undercurrents and tends, therefore, to be a rather fragile compromise formation. In spite of its fragility, however, when properly nourished and in full bloom, as it were, Reik sees love as having the capacity to transform one's emotional state almost as if by magic into a feeling of "salvation" following upon the sense of each in the pair having consummated an ideal in the love of each other.

According to Reik, falling out of love is initiated by the subject and not the beloved. De-idealization takes place and is followed by irritation, ill-will or indifference. But, apparently, not all is lost for, according to Reik, love is only possible because, he says, the sense of having lost at love creates the need, therefore, to re-find it. Apparently, then, there must have been some original love lost in order to make the need for love possible. Yet, unlike other analysts, Reik does not believe that narcissism stands in the way of love. He ascribes lack of self-confidence as the greatest hindrance to love.

Insecurities and lack of self-confidence get started in terms of the way the lover "reads" the reactions of his partner and follows from feelings of loss of independence and autonomy of will as a consequence of being so partnered. Discontent in the emotional state of the relationship is seen primarily, however, as stemming from unconscious guilt. Whereas love does not tolerate social anxiety and sweeps away guilt, nonetheless, accepting love without returning it, or feeling loved by the other while not loving oneself, produces guilt. Shyness can also produce the anticipation that the other will react negatively.

According to Reik, love has great social value because it is seen as having the power to overcome differences in class, race and creed. In addition, he believes sexual love creates happiness. Reik sums things up thusly:

> Romance is a nine day wonder. Love which would last undiminished through many years would be a miracle greater than those recorded in the Holy Scripture (p.189).

All and all, Reik's take on love represents a new and different picture. While he allows for sexual passion, he views the emotional state of love as a sort of social construct, limited, however, to the context of only one other person.

The emphasis on "re-finding" is not constructed theoretically as necessarily involving the more primitive relation to the mother's breast as much as it is the re-finding of the early state of bliss and omnipotence inherent in the ever present resonance of the early ego ideal.

REFERENCES

Freud, S. (1910) Contributions to the psychology of love. A special type of choice of object made by men. CP IV, 192–202.
——. (1912) Contributions to the psychology of love. The most prevalent form of degradation in erotic life. CP IV, 203–216.
——. (1931) Female sexuality. *C.P. V:*252–272.
Davis, R. (2002). Love escapes extinction. *Conference of the British Psychoanalytical Society, 2002.*
Green, A. (2002) Eros and Eris. *Conference of the British Psychoanalytical Society, 2002.*
Reik, T. 1949) *Of Love and Lust.* New York: Farrar, Strauss & Giroux.
Steiner, R. (2002) Freud on love: an historical overview. *Conference of the British Psychoanalytical Society,* 2002.

Chapter Six

Considerations on both
Male and Female Development

CONTEMPORARY NOTES ON FEMALE DEVELOPMENT

It is well known that Freud described the boy's oedipal struggle as involving the primal libidinal wish for the mother being frustrated by the fear of retaliation from the father, thereby forcing a separation from libidinal pursuit of the actual mother under the fantasized threat of castration by the father imago. Instead the boy chooses to save his penis and, in identification with it (and to reinforce its potency), he renounces his mother and, through identification with the father's phallus, is enabled to master his castration anxiety by choosing a substitute for his mother in the person of another not in competition with his father. The internalization of the fantasy of the prohibiting father creates an important part of the boy's "moral" super-ego.

As female psychosexual development does not involve a similar oedipalization, the little girl's super-ego is not as distinct in its specific form of principled renunciations and, in Freud's mind, is in some ways weaker in its regulating functions than the boy's super-ego. Yet, as has already been mentioned and discussed in previous chapters, the starting point for both girls and boys is the attachment to the original object of, in fantasy, the all powerful and nourishing mother, narcissistic identification with whom forms the basis for the primitive ego ideal which we have been talking about at length in relation to its function in falling in love. While for the boy the father also becomes implicated, via narcissistic identification, in the formation of a more mature aspect of his ego ideal, the little girl may see her father primarily as an erotic object she seeks to possess in order, by so doing, to obtain her wish for a penis she feels was denied her by her mother who, in fantasy (and according to Freud) she views as castrated, the same humiliating state she feels,

by identification, to have befallen herself as well. The incorporation of the father's penis is consolidated in the wish to have his "penis child."

Thus, for the boy the kernel of the neurosis is the complexity of resolving the Oedipus complex, but the same is not the case for the girl. The
framework underlying her neurotic vulnerability is constituted not in the
situation of the Oedipal complex, but more in the pre-oedipal phase leading
up to the oedipal situation. Hamon (2000), states that during the pre-
oedipal period the little girl perceives her mother as an object with a phallus. The discovery that she had been "castrated," as it were, turns the girl
away from the mother. Caught between the sense of being castrated like her
mother and looking for a way to avoid the narcissistic injury associated with
this psychic fact, the little girl solves the problem of the lack by creating a
fantasy of having a penis. Eventually, though, she gives this up for the fantasy of having the mother's penis in the form of her father and desires his
penis as a substitute for her own felt lacking of one. Thus the girl's narcissistic tie with the mother, via identification, is fraught by the conflict created by her wish to disidentify with her over this issue of resenting her
lacking a penis. The identification is fragile and fraught with anxieties just
as the little boy's development is fraught with his castration fears.

Hamon (2000) believes that the woman has no other way of recognizing
herself as a woman other than by relying upon, and trusting in, the good will
of her partner, a fact that retrospectively, as it were, suggests an increased
need to have depended upon the father (Sapichosin, 1999) seen as seductive.
But the seductive quality of the father is often interfered with by maternal
prohibition causing an identification with the father so as to safeguard a
needed safety from the threatening mother. (On this view the father, though
forbidding incest, nonetheless, gives a present to his daughter of offering
himself instead as desiring. This is an Ego gift governing lawless sexuality.)
The partial identification with the father gives the women an aspect of masculine narcissistic virility allowing her to achieve an active feminine sexuality allowing her the active pursuit of her male object. It also allows the fantasy of phallic potency potentially, in fantasy, endowing her with the trace of
sadistic identification formed in the fantasy of being castrated herself by
(rather than like) her mother. According to Hamon (2000), the woman's penis envy and its role in facilitating the sadistic fantasy of castrating her partner is an aspect of only part of her dynamics in loving, just as it had been in
her conflicted love of the castrated mother. Freud's last word, as it were, concerning the Oedipus complex was that it involved in both sexes the psychic
task of undoing maternal attachment. In boys he laid out the way in which this
created the conditions for the possibility of redirecting that love on mother
substitutes. It is Hamon's contribution, perhaps, to have noticed a similar dy-

namic in girls via their identificatory love of the father, to redirect some degree of libidinal attachment back onto the mother as well.

An interesting distinction has been made in discussing psychosexual differences between the sexes in terms of the character of the differences between male and female genitalia. The distinction is in terms of inside versus outside characteristics, male being more outside as it were and female being more inside. Kestenberg (1982) already observed in women that inner genital sensations with definite patterns and rhythms begin as early as the second year of life of the little girl, forming what she called an "inner core." Even earlier, Jones (1933) stated that girls have "inborn" sexual knowledge and innate oedipal fantasies. Stoller (1968), speaking of the same, coined the expression "core gender identity," and explained it in terms of learning by parental assignment. On this view, for example, women will be more preoccupied with relational issues relevant to their potential as mothers who need to "mother." This is not too surprising since the first attachment for a girl is an object of the same sex which, by identification, is established by a natural physical and psychological bond.

While Freud, essentially a physician and scientist, informed us that "anatomy is destiny", recent findings and observations have stimulated further comment on the differences between boys and girls based on the way they experience their bodies and their response to bodily sensations and feelings in relation to both the early and later developmental environments. Thus, Notman (2003) states that the role of physical development needs to be expanded to include object relations as well as cultural and personal meanings. Such exploration includes looking at somatic sensations in relation to affect:

> The way the body as a whole is experienced, in its family and cultural context as well as how specific parts of the body are represented consciously and unconsciously, has become the focus of much attention (p. 172).

The focus of her paper is the female body and its relationship to "femininity". Research of children has shown that sexual anatomical parts do not necessarily relate to gender, the later tending to be more confused and changeable. Children's awareness of their genitals and gender differences do not decide who is male and who is female. Is gender, then, a social construction? In her view, gender identity must be defined broadly, keeping in mind that there are many variations and ways of being masculine and feminine. Differences in patterns of interaction in boys and girls show that experience and its perception as a psychic matter can contribute to the activation of genes and, so, to the expression of a given genetic potential. Even brain structures are affected by experience.

There is a tendency in the literature to confuse female sexuality with female psychology. An important part of female body image is formed by such concepts as the experience of an 'inner' mysterious female structure whose function, thus latent meaning, is to be realized or performed 'later'. This, then, forms part of a female sense of self and is a component to the orientation of women to "waiting". The idea that feminine gender sense is partly constituted out of the nature of her reproductive role enhances this. Thus, pregnancy requires "waiting". Moreover, cultural expectations of passivity (of "waiting") can be seen to reinforce this attitude.

In female development, the girl's entire body contributes partly to her inner experience and its meaning. It is not only the awareness of her genitals but her awareness of her total body form. The attitude of the family determines whether her attributes are valued or devalued. For example, if a father tells his adolescent daughter who loves him that she is nothing but "a tall drink of water', the daughter feels devalued in her femininity and attractiveness. The mental representations include aspects of the way her body affects others and also her fantasies about the responses of others. Self-esteem and self-image arises partly out of the way communications from others are internalized. Moreover, "identifications can be consolidated around particular body characteristics that effect relationships with family members" (p. 579). Thus, for example, if a tall, lanky girl, when asking for a larger portion at dinner, is criticized by her father as having "eyes bigger than her mouth", she might interpret the message as meaning that her father is unwilling to grant her the sense competency to make her own decisions, as well as, perhaps, giving her the sense that he is a man who cannot give. Of course there are many more examples that could be given illustrating the many sub-cultural variations possible in determining the way body image is formed and internalized. Indeed, the way bodies are regarded and "coded", as it were, can vary widely from culture to culture with, in one culture, certain aspects of the body being accentuated while, in another, these same aspects being suppressed.

Bodily aspects unique to girls include the development of breasts. Unlike boys, at puberty, girls develop a new organ important both for sensual and reproductive functions. The bodily process of menses also distinguishes her development from male development. The pre-adolescent girl feels a sense of achievement when donning her first 'training' bra. At the same time, she may have conflicted feelings about it as she fears being compared to her mother whose breasts are fully developed in size and function. These feelings are associated in the girl at this difficult passage between being a girl and being a woman. Part of a girl's self-esteem is affected by this question of the size, shape and time of development of her breasts. An adolescent girl with large breasts may feel self-conscious while a girl with breasts she feels are too small may feel inadequate. Boys, too, may undergo similar issues of self-esteem in relation to the timely development and size of their reproductive organs. Indeed, for both sexes, the nature and function of their reproductive destiny determines, partly, the issues each will have in terms of self-esteem.

Without question, then, the idea of 'waiting', as part of her reproductive nature, contributes to female psychology and a woman's sense of "the feminine'. It also creates in women a greater tolerance than in men for ambiguous boundaries, part of an adaptive legacy, perhaps, arising out of the experience of pregnancy where the mother is both one with, and different from, her developing child. This may also account in part for the fact that for women the capacity for attachment and embeddedness in relationships is more acutely developed than it is in men. The capacity to 'wait' also allows women to transform rage, competition and aggression into self-criticism. For men this is a much more difficult achievement:

> The male's fear of woman, and his fear of the strength of his own wishes for attachment to the pre-oedipal mother; the regression that may accompany his wishes for attachment, and fear of being swallowed up or overcome, can produce a defensive devaluation of women by men. In their wish to please, women can perform to prevailing male views that are depreciating (p. 586).

On the other hand, female obesity can be a defense against sexuality and also provide a feeling of strength.

To better understand female sexuality, we need to make a distinction between sensuality and sexuality. Usually a love system desires to achieve two separate but related affect states: sensual enjoyment and sexual excitement. Sensual enjoyment has its roots in caretaking activities employed to soothe and express affection. It can lead to a diminution of tension or build up to sexual excitement. The latter refers to activities that lead to the enjoyment of orgasm. It is triggered in women by many of the care-giving activities mentioned above. But, according to Lazar and Lichtenberg (2003), sensual enjoyment is the more powerful motive force throughout the life cycle. It is so wide-spread in our lives that it is extensively made use of by the media, particularly in advertising.

In appreciating the importance of sensuality in this sense, what addition, we might ask, is contributed by 'femininity'? Each baby girl has biological givens that affect the unfolding of her gender identity. Sensory responses appear much earlier in girls and are well organized with greater mouth activity and tongue involvement in sucking. A mother may soon learn that that optimal arousal of a baby girl may come from gentler handling and that the greatest response comes from oral comforting. Even at twelve months of age, female infants are more sensitive to auditory signals than are boys and, during the course of development girls tend to be talked to more than are boys. It is also true that mothers maintain more physical closeness with baby girls than they do with male babies.

It has been found that femininity is well established by the end of the first year in the interplay between infant and family. Further distinction between genders is observed during the third year when both boys and girls react anxiously to observations of the genitals of the opposite sex. Around the third year, boys can be seen to chase girls who run away anxiously to their mothers, squealing and smiling. It is also around this age when little girls, upon seeing a small baby, react with delight and want to touch, hold and feel the infant. On the other hand, in boys, sexual activity is more intense and self absorbed than that of girls. The fingering of the male genitalia is direct and registers in the fingers and the eyes.

The use of thigh pressure in the girl is less clear and more diffuse. Vulva and clitoris are amenable to touch and pressure, but efforts to explore deeper in the vagina are apt to elicit pain. It is easier for the boy to associate his penis with thrusting, while the girl faces more difficulty in associating her vulva and clitoris with receptivity. However, on the other hand, the little girl develops an awareness of the potential of her genital area for engorgement, sensual enjoyment and sexual excitement. Perhaps reflecting a sense of vulnerability in being 'open', as it were, by the nature of their genitalia, studies show that, unlike boys, girls tend to prefer closed spaces. They were happy as they pursued their thoughts about the enclosed space they were experiencing in association with things female.

In noting how anatomical differences between the sexes are expressed in distinctive behaviors and fantasies, we need also to consider how the social environment reinforces the internalization of these differences. For example, while mothers may favor their son's autonomous activity, they tend to favor their daughter's sensitivity in their inter-relatedness. Interestingly, also, is the fact that whereas boys will react by withdrawing from a negatively expressive mother, feeling attacked and rejected, girls tend to remain within the adverse environment, increasing their skills in conflict responsiveness. Thus, girls get a dual message from their mother: they are rewarded if they distance themselves, but also get to feel the mother's more sensitive attachment when she is close and more related by more positively expressive affect. Little boys, on the other hand, not feeling equipped to handle mother's attacking , rejecting expression, may come away from the early environment with the mother feeling vulnerable to humiliating rejections by her, predisposing him in later life to form a self-protective hostility towards women, seriously compromising his capacity for intimacy.

But a universal femininity is basic to both sexes since the mother is the first person to give love and to be loved in return. In the area of sexuality, however, studies reflect differences between the sexes. For example, these studies indicate that women have a greater capacity than men for sexual and orgiastic functioning. Indeed, Sherfey (1966) reported that women experience a paradoxical state of sexual in-satiation in the moment of the utmost in sexual satiation. In her opinion female 'hyper-sexuality' was culturally repressed in the interest of the nuclear family. Based upon physiology, she concluded that women are far less suited to monogamy than men.

Person (1995), reports that the erotic life of men and women can also be quite different. For example, whereas men's fantasies are more impersonal based upon performance and domination, women's fantasies tend to be more romantic and include care-giving to others. Men use sexuality to shore up their gender identity while women's gender identity tends to derive from more varied sources. It is true, however, that women fear male strength and aggression. Their protective defenses may lead to masochistic accommodations and result in the compromising of authentic intimacy. Of course, such submission may herald identification with an idealized self-object; and merging with a strong male may serve the purpose of furthering, vicariously, a sense of power. The more intact and autonomous a women feels, however, the more she is able to relate with tenderness and intimacy in her erotic life.

Bernstein (1990) speaks of other psychic aspects resulting from the differences in the physiology of the sexes. For example, he notes the anatomical roots of certain female anxieties: fear of access, fear of penetration and fear of diffusivity. Women are afraid to close an opening, losing openness as a personality trait and losing pleasure. As already mentioned, women tend to compare themselves to other women concerning their bodies and particularly their breasts. Yet women often fear that other women might be envious and jealous and therefore often shrink from drawing attraction to themselves. In our society there is a new mandate to physical exercise in the service of perfecting the perfect body. Many women are obsessed with fat and diets, cosmetic surgery and liposuction. The focus on the body and its perfection has become a moral and ethical issue (Lieberman, 2003). The real shortage of suitable men to marry reinforces a wish for magical solutions. Such women want to be noticed and admired as a source of narcissistic supplies. Yet the obsession on body image may mask an underlying inner deadness or emptiness.

A good illustration of Bernstein's thinking is offered by Carolyn Ellman (2003) where she notes that a woman's reluctance to show her accomplishments may involve fears not only of masculine resentment, but also fears stemming from conflict rooted in the early mother-daughter relationship. Indeed, one of the essential differences between men and women is the importance of the mother relationship. While for men, as well as for women, the mother is a symbol of love and nourishment, the interpersonal and subjective experience of her is different for boys in relation to girls and vice-versa. For example, a man's fear of commitment is often traced to the fantasy of the early mother's seeming all-powerfulness and her capacity to reject by with-holding love if the little boy does not comply with her wishes. To defend against the fear of rejection, then, the man does not commit. The matter is much more complicated for women because their bodies are the same as their mother's. In an anthology of papers edited by this author, Fenchel (1998), various analysts focus on different topics highlighting the different aspects of the relationship between mother and daughter.

Sophie Freud speaks to the very fundamentals when she asks: "what is de-rived from mother for women"? She stresses that the mother has a more in-tensive narcissistic investment in a daughter than in a son. By the mother's self-absorption in her own self-doubts and feeling overly responsible for her product, mothers transmit female narcissism through generations. As women's survival depends upon loving and being loved, her self-confidence is gained by identifying with the libidinal resources of the female partner (the mother). In good enough female development, the girl has confidence that she will find a male partner in the world and to be loved by him the way she was loved by her mother and the way her mother (in fantasy) loved her father. The daughter's success, or lack thereof, effects the mother's self-esteem as she is so narcissistically invested in her daughter. As Bergman and Fahey (1998) point out, if a mother's frustrations with her daughter take over, the relation-ship devolves into a 'good'/'bad' dichotomy from which there is no easy res-olution and trauma to the daughter can result affecting her development.

Rosenberger (1998) elaborates further on the intricacies of the mother-daughter relationship by pointing out the effects that follow upon the fact that women are feared because of their sexual and reproductive powers. Thus, if maternal identification is with someone feared in this way, it poses a threat to her need to attach with a man who, in his fantasy, needs to be 'more powerful'. The other side of the coin is the power of the daughter's relational and attachment needs which, if the terms of the logic of the social-relational matrix are disrupted by too dramatic forces of social change, can create conflict causing her to feel the need to disidentify with the mother, creating shock waves to her self-agency. New and multiple models of womanhood in a diverse and pluralistic social matrix may in-deed foster conflict of the sort just mentioned resulting in the introduction of rigid defenses which actually may impair the daughter's capacity to adapt to new demands. Rosenberger (1998) suggests, as a possible solu-tion, the formation of a "bridging function" where the mother makes a meta-identification with "womanhood" in general that allows the daughter attachment by association rather than by replication.

The daughter's task of choosing a heterosexual partner becomes very complicated in this context as it depends upon the vicissitudes not only of the mother-daughter relationship, but also upon the quality of the parental marriage, the father's attitude towards women and the opportunities and roles society provides for women to express themselves. In this context, the social ideology of flaunting sexual freedom can create more conflict than that experienced in the ordinary adolescent crisis. Even in liberal homes girls can get quite a double message: they are to be discrete in their sexual activities, but active, curious and adventurous in all other areas. Moreover, the separation from the mother is much more difficult for girls than for boys because of body isomorphism between mother and daughter. An ill-defined sense of guilt stemming from the wish to be free from the mother may lead to unconscious punishment in the choice of partners. Success, it seems reasonable to say, requires an ego-organization not discouraged by the vagaries of love as internalized out of the conflicting messages emanating from family, society and culture. At best, heterosexual love is a complex attainment. In a culture of patriarchy, a wife may be satisfied that she has fulfilled her husband's needs while her satisfaction consists, in a sort of trickle-down fashion, by dint of her husband's personality and achievement, even though in his eyes she realizes that she has become more of a mother than a lover.

Maria Bergmann (1998) describes women who suffer from "role reversals". They need an exclusive dyadic relationship. By way of a quasi-parental preoccupation and seeming precocious identification with the maternal role, they are able to defend against sibling rivalry and exhibit a precocious altruism and seeming surrender to providing for the needs of the needy. Such precocious identification and role reversal with the mother, however, fosters incestuous guilt towards the father which, because not metabolized by the usual developmental internalizations limiting, by resolving, it, can result in a permanent source of internal conflict paid for by childlessness. Not surprisingly, such role-reversed women precociously identified with their mothers, develop strong defenses against fears of engulfment by their mothers and against fears of abandonment by either parent.

In a further elaboration, Mendell (1989) states that the Oedipal situation for such women has a completely different coloring, as it were, in relation to the way the father functions in it. In fantasy, the father becomes a sort of countermother instead of an independent male object. As discussed above, such women may find themselves needing to be involved with two men at the same time, in order to diffuse the enormous Oedipal guilt of being in such a close relationship with just one man (the father). In addition, however, the sexual desires for the father may also feel dangerous and fraught with fears of being abandoned by the mother. Moreover, under the influence of the defensive strategy of needing the male partner to be a sort of counter-mother rather than a separate male, these role-reversed woman's relationships with men get colored by their maternal transference which means conflicts between an intense wish for closeness, countered by an intense fear of re-engulfment, countered by an intense anxiety over separation and potential loss. Meanwhile, the degree to which any degree of intimacy is realized for such women in these sorts of relationships with men, is importantly derived, in large part, from the large component of "the feminine" projected onto such men and then identified with.

Women, however, get another opportunity to re-model the bond they share with their mothers when the latter is in her declining years and needs to be taken care of by their daughter. According to Adler (1998), the ill or aging mother undoes previously renounced bodily intimacies. Meanwhile, the adult woman devoted to caring for her dying mother can re-work earlier conflicts. But such a nurturing role can also mobilize intense aggression and force, by way of reaction formation, the need to repress these sadistic trends. "The daughter's close physical involvement with her mother's body is evocative. It rekindles early childhood feelings that offered the possibility of a reparative reunion with the care-giving mother of early infancy" (p.345).

Yet, as Klein pointed out much earlier, the enormous envy activated in this period may be defended against by the projection of an internally injuring mother creating, as Ellman notes, conflict over wanting what the mother has in relation to fears of punishment. This, then, sets off, later in life (and in relation to female peers), an anxious dialectic of merger and separation.

Such a constellation is buttressed by the fact that, early on, the mother does not recognize her daughter as a sexual being, but thinks of her, instead, as being unsatisfactory and incapable of satisfying. Meanwhile, the mother is experienced by the daughter as a powerful procreative being who has something the daughter lacks. Later on, this contributes to making the mother a dangerous and punishing rival to the little girl's oedipal wishes. To avoid this dangerous mother such women in later life may not allow themselves to have a mutually interdependent and equal relationship with a man, but may, rather, be overly meek and submissive, hiding their enormous resentment and envy. Thus, in an effort to hide their envy of the mother such women may condemn themselves to an-hedonic states of diminished happiness and excitement. Moreover, adding to these difficulties with men and complicating the picture even more, because, as suggested above, the little girl may have fostered considerable resentment towards the dangerous mother in this earlier pre-oedipal stage, when the daughter finally becomes interested in men and assumes her own procreative potential at the oedipal stage, she may experience herself in the fantasy of having become an oedipal victor over her mother (particularly in relation to a mother now in decline) and thus experience her former envy with shame and guilt. Such, of course, only adds to her difficulties in the sexual enjoyment of men.

Returning, however, to discussing the impact of sexual differences between men and women, Lasky (1990) wrote that arousal states are experienced differently in men as opposed to women. In both sexes there is tumescence, but in women it is experienced mostly as an internal matter accompanied by involuntary vaginal secretions. These sexual differences are based not only upon obvious visual cues, but more tellingly, perhaps, upon various activities of the body itself both internal and external. These body sensations are conditioned in part by the way in which the child relates to his or her own body in relation to its experience in terms of the mother. In this, the little boy is recognized by his mother as discontinuous with her body while the infant daughter is experienced as known and familiar by the mother in relation to her own body; which has a profound effect, as we have seen, upon the way the female infant comes to identify in relation to her mother. Kulish (1991) emphasizes that the interplay between perception and sensation in the context of the development of the body ego, contributes to early feminine gender identity. In this, the way the parents relate to and telegraph that reaction to the little girl has an important effect upon how she will relate to herself in this sense. Thus, the meaning conveyed by the parents in their reception of the facts of her genital endowment as either an absence (lacking a penis) or as a presence (having a vagina-clitoris) may have consequences in her self-understanding in this crucial regard as she matures. Kalinish (1993) saw such symbolic transmissions as sometimes responsible for neurotic lapses of memory in adult life.

There is also evidence that girls are very sensitive to the fluids in their bodies and have anxieties about being able to control them. Barnett (1966) compared the effects in the growing girl of the result of the anatomical fact of being able to control urethral and anal flows while being unable to do so with her menstrual flow. Unlike boys, her sexual excitement is felt but unseen, keeping her arousal a private matter. Merging with other pleasurable sensations over her entire body, the genital arousal of the girl results in the libidinization of her entire body, making her genitals a highly prized possession. The relationship between sexuality and love occurs earlier in women than in men. But women, in contrast to men, have more issues with dependence and the wish to be dependent in relation to the question of feeling in control of another. Women are more concerned with empathy. Limitations to the feeling of love or non-attunement in the feeling of such can be experienced as betrayal or as being let down.

Self-esteem issues in women can result not only from developmental problems involved in the process of intra-psychic consolidation and development, but also as the result of conflict in the realm of the relation of the maturing girl to her external environment as well (Loewald, 1960). Lack of sense of continuity and integration with the environment may give rise to the development of a narcissistic ego ideal which will have important effects in influencing a woman's growing sense of gender identity. Whereas initially differences between the sexes will be denied because of devaluation of the female parent, later on these devalued parents may become the model for self-understanding and integration creating conflicts in self esteem resulting from the concealed devaluation. Feelings and actions stemming from an ego ideal that incorporates aspects of an ambivalently cathected parent, may result in self-destructive patterns that manifest themselves as attacks on thinking. Shame, humiliation and embarrassment prevail. If the mother of the little girl possesses these traits herself, the little girl may attempt to safeguard her self-esteem by trying to be like her father. Such defensive measures, however, often result in the development of a false self (Fenchel, 1987).

When identifications clash with counter-identifications, the priority becomes avoiding pain. This has important effects upon moral development. There occurs a shift from need satisfaction to a psychology of how to accommodate one's own wishes to internalized ideals. Because values derive their stability from complimentary identifications, the internalization of prohibitions from harshly critical external objects often create obstacles to smooth superego integration and may result in acting out in behaviors including, for example, petty thefts and shop lifting. Such counter-identifications are difficult to dislodge because of their sexually gratifying nature. Nonetheless, Loewald (1960a) strongly counsels that for change in function to occur with such persons, these harsh introjects need to be externalized and worked through in the context of transference analysis in analytic treatment.

CONTEMPORARY NOTES ON MALE DEVELOPMENT

Freud's theories of male psychosexual development are well known. Since then other voices have been heard that amplify and elaborate the Freudian account. Munder Ross (2000) questions that masculine development proceeds as linear as has thus far been suggested. He conducted research studies of children ranging in ages from 3–10 years of age and found that early on boys do not show aspects of masculine pride associated with identification with the father since, in reacting to the effects of the fantasy of the all-powerful mother who is believed as solely responsible for the fact of reproduction, boys perceive men as barren having lost their penis during coitus. The woman is seen as a force not unlike that in the depiction of woman as an ancient fertility goddess, while the father's role, in contrast, remains in the shadows and is ill-defined. Around the age of five years, however, the maternal identification gives way to an illusionary patriarchy when it is first understood that men help in making babies and in their caretaking as well. At this point, children begin to integrate both male and female identifications. If gender roles stay fluid and do not become rigid (permitting, therefore, identifications with feminine aspects as well) male development can proceed in a way productive of a stable and mature masculine identity.

Falling in love, a late adolescent occurrence, represents another developmental achievement or task for boys. In this, the young man now has to identify with his father and the father's superego. Thus, Munder Ross (2000) writes:

> With intimate love the mortality of early childhood is replaced with the "ethics" of the adult (p.65).

Love is blind and its regressive dynamics can endanger barely achieved developmental consolidations and pose threats to those integrations that provide the young man with a sense of an existing value system and the security it offers. It can also be challenging to his existing ego-ideal and the function it plays in helping him to turn away from his mother and feel comfortable in his masculinity. The love object rekindles forbidden oedipal wishes and provokes the activation of more archaic wishes for transgression in something "forbidden." If these temptations are to be overcome, the young man must learn to relinquish his rivalry with his father and accept in himself what is instinctual including, perhaps, bisexual currents as well.

According to Munder Ross (2000), the young man invests his sexual partner with some of his father's authority internalized and projected as part of his projected ego ideal as well. If this proceeds too far, however, the man may lose his desire for the woman, but if successful, the projection of the ego ideal onto the beloved prepares the man to introject aspects of her feminine values. This leads to an alteration of his super-ego, the site of his ego ideal, and allows for modifications that include the introjection of the woman's less uncompromising and more merciful modes of judging. Indeed, according to Ross, there is a need in all men to want to be like women in some respects in addition to wanting to be men. After all, men begin their emotional life with a woman with whom they identify. Only later with the discovery of the father in the need to separate from the all powerful mother, do boys become more attuned to the masculinity of the father which is often associated with aggression and, hence, with an awakening experience of their own aggression. Most men are terrified by awareness of the potential for violence inherent in some of the dynamics fantasized and real in their complex relation to the father and need modification of such harshness by acceptance of counterbalancing feminine identifications.

For Jonathan Lear (1991), the instincts themselves are modified by love through the process of acceptance and understanding of our need for loving. According to Lear, this involves developing a loving and responsive relation to our drives, something he says happens when we fall in love. Love in action becomes a process incorporating the natural forces of drives, themselves a manifestation of love, and transforming them in the process by the internalizations facilitated in the responses they encounter in the process of being loved in return.

Midlife provides another opportunity for insight in understanding male development. Diamond (2004), suggests that men harbor gender "enigmas" that midlife provides an opportunity for reconciliation and integration of by allowing the transformation and amelioration of phallic fantasies rooted in a more one-sided masculinity. Disagreeing with Freud's idea of linear sexual development, Diamond suggests, instead, that ambiguities of gender are continuously reworked across different developmental stages and are shaped by crucially important life experiences. For example, he sees an important transition occurring between the ages, roughly, of forty to fifty-four. In the event, an actual midlife crisis develops involving arrested adult development caused by narcissistic injury arising out of the unique way the individual has internalized conflict over masculine and feminine identifications to date. When overcome and worked through, a more profound sense of interiority can develop in the man as a greater harmony is established in relation to previously unintegrated psychic representations and identifications in the context of a growing realization and acceptance of the fact that biological decline is unmistakable and death is no longer an abstract possibility. With disengagement from internalized conflict derived from more archaic conflicts with the early environment, there occurs a growing acceptance of an increased capacity for receptivity, affiliation and nurturing; in short, there is an effort to integrate the internal feminine.

Diamond opposes Freud's notion that the boy "disidentifies" with the mother in the rather one dimensional and "masculinist" sense implied by his version of psychosexual development. Instead, Diamond suggests a more subtle dialectic of disavowal and denial where the little boy is seen as identifying with the mother in his internalization of how she relates to his masculine body and its internalized psychic representations. Diamond sees identification issues developing out of conflict when aspects of internalizations and identifications with the father become in conflict with the maternal identifications. Such conflicts become intensified if paternal identifications are experienced as internalizations of harsh, "masculinist" introjects in the father. In contrast, where the father is seen and felt as more attuned and loving of his wife and accepting of his own feminine identifications and needs, the little boy is able to internalize a more flexible masculinity. As a consequence, the little boy's need to separate from his mother is experienced with less sense of traumatic loss.

Because the masculine ego ideal is created in terms of the struggle the little boy experiences during his initial stages of gender differentiation, and in a culture where there is considerable pressure on males to renounce inconsistent gender traits, the narcissistic injury experienced in the loss of the maternal self is often defended against in the little boy by flight to identification with an all powerful phallic other. This, of course, creates a very harsh oedipal phase in the encounter with the father and internalization of a harsh superego and corresponding activation of primitive aggression disrupting the effects that love might bring to such an inharmonious integration. On the other hand, this flight to the phallic remains in the unconscious as symbol of reunion with the mother, therefore ameliorating the boy's sense of traumatic separateness from her by substituting an increased sense of influence over her (while, at the same time, as above, upping the ante in overcoming later oedipal conflict.) If this were not enough, however, Diamond also suggests that the cultural dismissal of male interiority, and with it the dismissal of a certain degree of feminine resonance in the male psyche, is a factor in the formation of male penetration anxieties.

To conclude this section, both Diamond and Ross in representing new theoretical perspectives on male development, agree that it is important to the development of harmonious male identity that both genders be represented and accepted in the identificatory structure of the developing male psyche. Christian David (1970) has observed that resistance to seeing the crucial import of such heterogeneity in male psychic development stems in no small part from the fact that until recently, "many analytical conceptions of femininity [have been] themselves the stronghold of fantasies and the last refuge of prejudices" (p. 17), one of the most destructive of such prejudices being the view that the active aspect of femininity is really only a reaction formation against feeling a deficient man. Short of sociological and cultural pressures to repress opposite sex identifications, bisexual identifications occur naturally in the development of both sexes making sexual difference less rigid by allowing into consciousness an appreciation for the fact, as Groddeck (1961) said, that in every male there is something feminine or "female," while in every female there is something masculine or "male." Moreover, because it seems that a more lucid and detailed recognition of this duality at the heart of identity would allow sexual life that, because more genuine, was more open and more free, there seems much to recommend this view.

REFERENCES

Adler, H. Ministering to the dying mother. In: *The Mother-Daughter Relationship.*
    G. Fenchel (ed), p. 329–348. Northvale, N.J.: Aronson, 1998.

Barnett, M. (1966) Vaginal awareness in the infancy and childhood of girls. *Journal
    of the American Psychoanalytic Association, 14:*129–141.

Bergman & Fahey. Some thoughts on the creation of character. In: *The Mother-
    Daughter Relationship.* G. Fenchel (ed), p. 29–43, Northvale, N.J.: Aronson, 1998.

Bergmann, M. The effect of role reversal on delayed marriage and maternity. In: *The
    Mother-Daughter Relationship,* G. Fenchel (ed), p. 173–194. Northvale, N.J.:
    Aronson, 1998.

Bernstein, D. (1990) Female genital anxieties, conflicts and typical mastery modes.
    *International Journal of Psycho-Analysis, 71:*151–165.

David, C. (1970) A Masculine Mythology of Femininity. In: Chasseguet-Smirgel, *Fe-
    male Sexuality—New Psychoanalytic Views,* pp. 17—67. Ann Arbor, University of
    Michigan Press, 1970.

Diamond, M.J. (2004) Assessing the multitude within: a psychoanalytic perspective
    on the transformation of masculinity at mid-life. *International Journal of Psycho-
    Analysis, 85:*45–64.

Ellman, C.S. (2003) Women's fear of being envied. *Round Robin, 18,* Spring 2003.

Fenchel, G.H. (1987). Clinical interventions in character analysis: the ego ideal and
    the superego value system in analysis. *Issues in Ego Psychology, 10:*46–50.

Groddeck, G. (1961) *The Book of the It.* New York: Funk & Wagnall.

Hamon, M. C. (2000) *Why Do Women Love Men and Not Their Mothers?* New York:
    The Other Press.

Jones, E. (1933) The phallic phase. *International Journal of Psycho-Analysis,
    14:*1–33.

Kalinish, L. (1993) On the sense of absence: a perspective on womanly issues. *Psy-
    choanalytic Quarterly, 62:*206–227.

Kestenberg, J. (1982) The inner genital phase: Pre-phallic and pre-oedipal. In *Early
    Female Development,* ed. D. Mendell. New York: S.P. Medical and Scientific
    Books, 71–126.

Kulish, L. (1991) The mental representation of the clitoris: the fear of female sexual-
    ity. *Psychoanalytic Inquiry, 11:*511–536.

Lasky, R. (1990) Body ego and the pre-oedipal roots of feminine gender identity.
    *Journal of the American Psychoanalytic Association, 48:*1381–1412.

Lear, J. (1991) *Love and Its Place in Nature.* Chicago: Noonday Press.

Lieberman, J. (2003) On looking and being looked at. *Round Robin, 18,* Spring 2003

Loewald, H. (1960) Ego and reality. *Papers on Psychoanalysis.* New Haven: Yale U.
    Press.

———. (1960a) The problem of defense and the neurotic interpretation of reality. *Pa-
    pers on Psychoanalysis.* New Haven: Yale University Press.

Mendel, D. The impact of the mother-daughter relationship on women's relationships
    with men: The two men phenomenon. In: *The Mother-Daughter Relationship.*
    G. Fenchel (ed), p. 227–240. Northvale, N.J.: Aronson, 1998.

Notman, M. (2003) The female body and its meanings. *Psychoanalytic Inquiry,* *23*:572–591.

Person, E. (1995). *By Force of Fantasy.* New York: Penguin Books.

Ross, M.J. (2000) What do men want? *Issues in Psychoanalytic Psychology.* *22*:53–68.

Sapisochin, G. (1996) Paper presented to the Madrid Psychoanalytical Association, 1996.

Sherfey, M.J. (1966) The evolution and nature of female sexuality in relation to psychoanalytic Theory. *Journal of the American Psychoanalytic Association,* *14*:28–128.

Stoller, R.J. (1968) *Sex and Gender.* Maresfield Library; London: Karnac Books, 1984.

Chapter Seven

Cultural Influences on the Development of Love

LOVE AS AN EXPRESSION OF CULTURE

Different cultures espouse different mythologies about love. Persian romanticism, exemplified in the verses of Omar Khayyam, offers one such cultural outlook. Then there are the views contained in Hindu religion with gods (like the goddess Kali, for example, both a fertility goddess and a destroyer), who can be sexy, evil and tricky all at the same time. Meanwhile, the Judaic tradition in producing the well known "Song of Songs" celebrates both love and sensuality. In all cultural traditions we find that love and how it is practiced is prescribed by the unique set of sanctions and taboos that define each such culture. Since sexuality is a companion of love, we find it regulated in different ways by different cultures as well in order, presumably, to prevent social chaos.

Yet there are certain fantasies and themes about creation and death and life and sexuality that appear common to all cultures from the Australian Aborigine to Native Americans to our own present "Western" culture as well. On the other hand, rituals and social mechanisms erected to defend against certain unconscious fantasies are varied. Michele Stephen (2003) claims, however, that our understanding of the differences between different cultures and societies should not be reduced simply to a conception of differing defenses erected in relation to unconscious desires since, she says, cultures are better understood more as "intricate webs of meanings, explicit, implicit and hidden" (p.616). Yet, as the following brief illustration suggests, it seems that we cannot leave out the unconscious in explaining cultural rites and rituals. In New Guinea, for example, initiation rites for young men carry the implication that women are dangerous and are to be avoided because they "pollute" (menses) and poison. Strength is to be drawn from other men by ingesting their semen via homosexual practices such as fellatio. Underlying the motivation for such rituals is the fantasy of an "Ur-mother" who, incorporating aspects of both sexes with the power to both create and destroy life, is all powerful and, therefore, needing defense against. She is defended against by ritualistically becoming separate from her through the ingesting of semen, the essence of the power of masculinity. As such, she underlies the displacement from the milky life giving discharge from the breast to the milky discharge from the penis in the condensation of the "penis breast." It seems, then, that we can not leave out the unconscious in our understanding of culture and that, therefore, it is probably true to say that, in all generality, culture is the outcome of an interplay between unconscious needs and desires in relation to biological and environmental forces.

Now, as life begins in birth and ends in death, we would expect that just as love is accounted for in mythology so, also, is death in need of accounting for. We know this to be the case since we know that through the ages mythology is the way mankind has attempted to answer the perennial questions of the truth, meaning and significance of life that begins in birth and ends in death. Mythology is the answer to the need to touch upon the eternal and mysterious in our effort to find out who we are. As Campbell (1988) said, mythology is the response to the need to resonate "with our innermost being and reality, so that we actually feel the rapture of being alive" (p.5).

Freud expressed an opinion of how to understand the meaning of culture in different ways. For example, in *Civilization and Its Discontents* (1930) he spoke about the struggle between Eros and Thanatos and while he hoped that Eros could sustain itself, he expressed some uncertainty about whether it would: "But who can foresee with what success and with what result [the outcome between these two forces]" (P.145). He saw a continuing potential for cultural malaise and war which he thought unpreventable in the near future as men had not given up their animalistic past. It might be said that Freud occupies a middle ground in thinking about the likely outcome in the struggle between Eros and Thanatos between Hobbes (an inquiry into the basis of social life that sees it as the outcome of a contract with a strong sovereign in which individuals give up a certain degree of autonomy in order to be protected from the appetites of their fellow men) on the more pessimistic side and Hegel (antagonism can be overcome and freedom secured if fulfillment is sought in social life) on the more optimistic side.

Freud (1913) gives some hints in his paper "On Transience," where he bemoans the fact that people are unable to love the short-lived sense of libidinal integration evoked out of recognition of, and sympathetic vibration with, the beauty of nature because of conflict generated out of a defensive flight from mourning. Drassinower (2003) amplified on this theme by stating that the denial of death and the flight from mourning inevitably leads to war. Freud left no clear "road map" taking us out of this dilemma. Freud seemed to think that "malaise" grew out of the cultural forms of political and religious authority that demanded strict obedience while leaving little room for individual, creative (libidinal) judgment (mediation).

Drassinower (2003) bases his ideas on the concept of psychoanalysis as a form of adult re-education. Rejection of infantile nostalgia and the capacity to say "No" opens up the possibility of an "erotic" social life based on a more libidinally configured intersubjectivity. Accepting the negative and finiteness of life (and, thereby, to allow mourning of the sense of loss to narcissistic wholeness) makes it possible to love those close to us in spite of disappointment in our limitedness.

Somewhat reminiscent (in emphasis) to the work of Joseph Campbell and in reaction to Freud as well, Person (2004) believes that any informative discussion of psychoanalysis must include reference to cultural myths and their meanings. In this, she speaks not so much of a "collective unconscious," but of a "cultural unconscious" in which the drive for "power" is the motivating underlying force, much as the Freudian concepts of "sex" and aggression underlie and constitute the dynamics of the Freudian model. Thus, for example, according to Person, the so-called sexual and gender liberation movements have revealed the extent to which hidden hierarchical biases underlie and influence the ways in which a given culture comes to cast what is meant to be "male," "female," "gay" or "straight," often exposing not so subtle power agendas implicit in the order of ranking. Thus she sees the need to locate "power" at the center of any critical psychoanalytic self-understanding when applied in the context of socio-cultural understanding.

Her concept of the 'cultural unconscious' is formulated as the outcome of a process of socialization in which the dominant socio-cultural precepts of a given society become internalized (at first through the family and then more generally through one's "extra-family" experience of society) as the self-regulatory system ordering the sense of well being and self-acceptance at the heart of an individual's sense of identity. Unlike Freud's system which she sees as unnecessarily time bound to his own time, she sees her own analytic as applicable to any time without taint by more historically-limited, prejudicial, normative assumptions. She stresses that it is in our first encounter with the family hierarchy in a state of dependence, that we first learn the dynamics of power in shaping who we are and what our place is within that family system. It is here that we first learn to negotiate, as we are affected by, various different and simultaneously intersecting power grids both within and beyond the family in which we try to find a niche within which we can dwell in some degree of balance and peace. At any given point in our encounter with, and adaptation to, these various power grids, however, the degree of power we achieve for ourselves will depend upon our psychology, our development and our age. Culture, she states, discriminates against the very young and the very old.

Person makes a reference to Arlow (1951) who states that myth provides an umbrella for multiple, sometimes conflicting needs to be integrated within a single, accepted cultural script. And while such myths often preserve the status quo, they may also, under certain circumstances, lead to cultural change when, for example, a group of people come to re-imagine "the social" out of a response to a changing cultural milieu. More often, though, such changes occur as a result of the pressure of political activists who become spokespersons for the dreams and hopes of a new generation or of other such disenfranchised groups. The new organizing myth then becomes internalized and acted upon as though it were one with "reality." Thus, the Freudian view that adaptation to reality is a relation in terms merely of the outcome of intra-psychic conflict and defense defined narrowly in terms of integrations of libidinal and aggressive "drives," needs to be modified to include the important role that culture plays in shaping the developmental process in terms of the changing dynamics generated out of intra-psychic conflict and defense.

How dependent definitions and expressions of love are on society and its then present culture is clearly to be seen in some of our best known dramas and operas. For example, the great German poet Goethe wrote his masterpiece *Faust* which was later translated into an opera by the French composer Gounod. The original play came in two parts. The first part deals with an aging philosopher near the end of his life who wishes to be rejuvenated so as to understand all of the mysteries of the universe. In order to accomplish this, he makes a pact with the Devil whereby he agrees that if the Devil will rejuvenate him as he wishes, the Devil may have his soul. Rejuvenated, Faust no longer thinks of death and, having regained his youth, sets out on a path to experience all his passions to their fullest.

Now, of course, as this is against the natural order of things as well as in conflict with theology, his transformation may be seen as an attempt to overcome the limits and boundaries of reality for those of fantasy. The second part of the play deals with what happens to Faust after his passions have wreaked him and caused the death of the woman with whom he fell in love. Of course, there must follow atonement if there is to be salvation. (Apparently, as death approaches we must turn to and embrace God if we are to be saved for another world, the world of Paradise.)

Now interestingly, there are also some mutterings that Faust is required to return as well to the "the world of the Mother". This involves a second transformation, for as he caused the death of the woman he loved, so he must repair his sin by confronting the "primordial woman (Mother)". Only by passing this ordeal will his sin be cleansed so that he may be saved. Indeed, towards the end of the second part of the play we are told of bells ringing announcing Faust's salvation and redemption. Moreover, in the coda of the play is announced the slogan: "only hard work will redeem us"! The moral of this morality play is that there is a price to pay for indulging our narcissism and passions; and if we transgress the law only virtue and hard work will save us. But, more than that, the coda of the play seems also to exclaim that atoning for one's sins also requires a return to an eternal feminine — a suggestion, perhaps, that phallic narcissism is a defense against a more archaic wish to regress to a more symbiotic narcissistic oneness with the mother. Thus both Freud and Klein hypothesize: *Das ewig weibliche zieht uns heran!?*

Grand opera provides another means of expression of the Zeitgeist. And again, it is German culture that speaks to us forcefully. As Goethe in his time spoke for literature, Richard Wagner became the spokesman for the operatic stage. Themes of love, hate and betrayal come repeatedly to our attention. Who, for example, has not heard of *Tristan un Isolde?* In the beginning, they were enemies and then, low and behold, romantic love draws them to each other just as fiercely as enmity had previously done so. But here too, there is a price to pay. Tristan must die, but unlike Goethe's Faust, there seems to be no salvation in the bargain.

The influences of romanticism and paganism versus Christianity are found expressed in Wagner's greatest of operatic achievements; namely, *The Ring of the Nibelung*, considered by many the greatest music dramas ever composed. When Wagner began the *Ring* he was influenced by the philosopher Ludwig Feuerbach who believed that Man created God in the sense that religion is merely the expression of Man's needs and that its most meaningful revelation is that God is love. Literally, then, according to Feuerbach, the pathway to salvation is love. Toward the end of the Ring, however, Wagner seems to have been more influenced by the more pessimistic philosophy of Schopenhauer; thus, the destruction of Valhalla and Wotan's personal abdication.

In many respects, the theme of this colossal work is the dismissal of both the God of Judaism as well as the God of Christianity. Without either such God, there is no creator and the world is polytheistic and polymorphous. Though Wotan is the chairman of the board, as it were, the gods run around like adolescents, rampant with lusty passion. Even in the beginning of the cycle, Alberich and the Rhinemaidens cavort seductively and lasciviously. We are told that Alberirch will foreswear true love and concentrate instead upon sexuality and power. This is also the attitude of the gods in their relationship to earthlings and, indirectly, their relationships to each other as well. Wotan has promised the goddess Freya to the giants from the world of the giants in exchange for their labor in constructing the impenetrable castle of *Valhalla.* But he has no intention of fulfilling his promise since Freya, by way of the magic of her golden apples, is essential to keep the gods rejuvenated and forever young.

Wotan expects that his illegitimate son, Sigmund, will recover the gold stolen by the Nibelung Alberich which is stored under the protection of a fierce dragon. The gold will be paid to the giants in lieu of Freya. Unfortunately, Sigmund falls in love with Siglinde who unbeknownst to him was fathered by the busy Wotan and is therefore Sigmund's sister. Yet even when he finds out, the fear of incest does not stop Sigmund. Thus Wagner presents a world without the constraints of the Decalogue and a society where paganism, sensuality, fighting and thievery all intermingle; where order is loosely maintained by treaties arranged by Wotan himself.

Yet, even though the polymorphous-perverse predominates the work, there is, nonetheless, throughout the whole cycle, from the dawn of consciousness to the obliteration of the entire cosmic order, a compelling moral order. Powerful Wotan himself is not all knowing and must seek advice from others. He is also bound by his treaties and those of the other gods. He must obey the law. So after the beginnings of Sigmund's budding, incestuous romance he sends his daughter (the Valkyrie) to try and protect Sigmund, his son, from a fated fight with Hundig, Siglinde's father. But Fricka, Wotan's wife, informs Wotan that she is Hundig's protector (as protectress of marriage and the hearth and home) and that it is Sigmund who must die. She tells Wotan that if he is to continue to rule, he must obey the law. So depressed and not liking Fricka's constraints, he decides to kill both Sigmund and Hundig.

Now *The Ring,* like *Faust,* had an enormous impact on the thinking of the day. Romanticism and classicism were at war as was paganism and Christianity. But romantic love as well as sexual love played an important part in these stories. Such love, however, was usually unrewarded (unrequited) or punished. It is interesting to note, however, that in his later years, Wagner thought love could be a source of ultimate redemption. In his scheme of things love starts off as sexual love but then tempers into the love of children, brothers, sisters, friends and, finally, into the universal love of humanity. The point of this rather long digression, then, is that cultural myths and stories help to create the atmosphere within which love is regulated in such a way as to inform us both of the importance of lust and love and of its transformative power, as well as to constrain us in our uninhibited expression of such love and lust lest we be punished for our moral transgressions by church and or state.

Although discussion of the role culture and myth plays upon the identity and intra-psychic harmony of an individual is important to keep in mind, this fact seems a long way from the exploration of 'love' that we are so dedicated to elaborate. Yet, such excursions into the dimension of "the socio-cultural," as it were, are essential since love is, by definition, a social enterprise occurring within a cultural context. However, any exploration of 'love' will undoubtedly be hampered by the use of words that have so many varied meanings. While human beings are unique in using language as a means of communication, words portray only one kind of reality while subtexts created out of the negative spaces left by our words portray another. Benda (1961) says that consciousness consists in the interpretation of data and the meaning assigned to such data through the use of words that, in and of themselves, have meaning only in their use in designating (through their interrelations in a particular usage) a specific view or explanation of life. In this, their intrinsic function is reference outward from an inner "private" realm to an outer (or public) realm. Language, consisting as it does in this use of words to describe and explore "objects", has this "public" feature as intrinsic to its dialogic function. That is, language is possible only because it functions as the consequence of the need for conversational (or dialogic) relatedness between two parties.

To circumvent semantic difficulties, Lear (1991) suggests that "love" is a form of nature and is embedded in the need for sensual connection (appreciation) between the world and ourselves. This same notion was expressed by Slavin (2002) who coined the phrase "innocent sexuality." We need to remember that love as defined by the Church in the Middle Ages did not even include the notion of a special relationship with another unique person. The focus was upon the idea of "agape" or spiritual love, mostly disembodied. Eros, sexual romantic love, was downgraded by the church to mere biological urge. It was only with the troubadours and Minnesingers that a more individualized romantic love was rescued from its neglected stance by the monolithic system of the church. In those days, emphasizing the importance of individual feelings and sentiments over those of a church dominated society was a novel, frightening and threatening development.

According to Gargiulo (1987) because superegos and ego ideals are not only received from the parents but are also transmitted by the cultural media reflecting the means and distribution of power in the society, the quality of loving often reflects the degree of conflict resolution implicit in the compromise formation that defines the degree of resolution and integration of conflict implicit in a particular culture at a given time. Thus, for example, although he makes a case for obsessive loyalty in anal-sadistic cultures, one can also make the case for envious competition as a trait of consumerist society arising out of the sense of entitlement implicit in a narcissistically structured culture such as ours where grandiose fantasies proliferate. At the same time others in our culture are driven by the fable of the "self-made man" suggesting that by dint of honest, hard work over long hours selflessly pursued for one's own betterment, the system will reward one with whatever one wished for. Of course, this is to a large extent an illusion leaving out the fact that what often drives success is dishonesty, manipulation and the incalculable influence of the "right connections." Moreover, where the sense of vulnerability to the harshness of "the system" is greatest, as in Ghetto culture, the emphasis is upon acquiring power by whatever ruthless means necessary in order not to be taken advantage of by one's rivals. It should not be surprising, then, that in such cultures where the logic of exploitation is upper most, love relationships are likewise skewed by the same dynamics.

It would seem that in our present society man feels dehumanized and mechanized in relationship to both his internal and external world. As his identity has become fragmented there seems to be no more an important issue than the avoidance of frustration and the need for instant gratification in lieu of the certainty of economic well being. Very few are able to get behind values or causes that require looking beyond one's own selfish perspective. Fragmented and lonely, individuals become separate from a sense of belonging to a supportive and nurturing community forged out of sympathetic understanding of needs common to the human condition. Under such limited scope for human relatedness outside of oneself, falling in love becomes the only hope. But is this the only hope? In a discussion about the future (IPTAR, 1969), Herbert Marcuse was cited as suggesting that because, in an affluent society such as our own, there is the potential for technology to replace repression, there can be a diminution in the harshness of the reality principle by substituting a less repressive one, more allowing of libidinal needs and their expression. On his view, the idea of the reality principle as a permanent, unchanging fact beyond our control is an ideological fiction born of the logic of surplus repression implicit in the capitalistic mode of production that defines the economic formation of our times. Instead, he sees the possibility of a non-repressive reality principle reconfigured to be more in confluence with the pleasure principle of early life.

Even granting this argument, however, it is important to point out that when early pain and frustration predominate to such an extent, the pleasure principle not withstanding, the objects necessary to sustain relatedness and gratification become tainted and psychic resources become mobilized in the service of avoiding recognition of reality. Regressive dynamics predominate and, as Gordon (1969) points out, anxiety and fears of annihilation propel people toward the wish for merging experiences in a fantasized undifferentiated, larger whole. She concluded:

> The question may be raised whether some of the regressive activity may prove serviceable to the ego and may result in new cultural symbols appropriate to the

current state of civilization. And if these symbols take the magical power of the unrepressed infantile psyche and symbiotic union with the mother, as Freudians, we should not be surprised (p.11).

Even the quality of falling in love is different at different stages in the life cycle. Love and sexuality appear simultaneously in human existence as a developmental challenge that has to be met. The deck is loaded, however, against the attainment of a successful relationship. And here again there is the intruding influence of culture and the conflicts engendered by the relation between these values and the drive to sexual gratification. If, for men, the goal is to be all powerful so as to be in charge, as it were, sexuality can be part of a fantasy of conquest, competition and contest. If women, on the other hand, are not confident in their core gender identity and need men to reflect aspects of their own femininity (men, that is, who are so disidentified with their own identificatiory femininity that their identity is defensively skewed by the need for over-identification with phallic power), a conflicted dynamic ensues dooming the possibility of harmonious relatedness and setting in motion the seeds for sado-masochistic dynamics of dehumanization. Although some place the blame for such dynamics squarely upon the shoulders of culturally induced conflict, such sweeping placement of blame forgets the fact that the super-ego is modifiable in terms of the internalization of corrective emotional experience in the form of the libidinal quality of the unique experience of unique individuals in the context of repeated sexual coupling. Moreover, the effects of rigid super ego interference to libidinal gratification (in one's love life, for example) are modifiable in the context of analytic treatment.

CULTURE AND SEXUALITY

Just as has been observed in the case of 'love's' being influenced by cultural factors, so too is desire and sexual performance influenced by conflicts engendered when desire comes in conflict with core values embedded in the culture in the context of ontogenetic imperatives following from the dictates of ontogenetic development. As we have observed, because of the nature of sexual desire, and its need constantly to be renewed by "the new," romantic relationships of any lasting degree often flounder and come apart. Indeed, its not enough to be beautiful in the eyes of the beholder. It is necessary as well to be part of the fantasy of re-finding something unattainable; therefore, to be something awakening the relish for consummation of the desire to be reunited with this forever lost original object. Once the current object no longer holds out the possibility for such reunion (impossible since by definition the object of such union is unattainable) disillusion with the current object sets in and, without its capacity to enchant, gets discarded for the next one that, while reawakening the same fantasy, nonetheless, holds out but the same doomed promise. And so it goes. Moreover, another aspect in such love relations tending to defeat their longevity is the potential of emotional conflict supervening, as it were, over the sexual subtext negating its importance altogether. We see this often in couples who, no longer trusting one another to have their best interests at heart, are no longer interested in sexual union no matter how physically attractive each, in an objective sense, should be to the other.

All things being equal, though, and where development has proceeded normally, there is a period of innocent sexuality which is adventurous, playful and libidinal (outside the sphere of conflict) that holds out the promise of unending gratification and pleasure (Slavin,2002). Otto Fenichel (1945) recognized this same phenomenon when he described the corresponding emotional component to such innocent sexuality as consisting in the fantasy of each lover respecting the vulnerability of the other in the wish to gratify one another with the aim of maximizing each other's pleasure. Why should this discovery be surprising? After all, when we speak about love or sex, we are speaking about a universal desire human beings have in relating towards one another for these most basic needs, the need for love and gratification. Why, then, should it be so hard to attain such in practice? Consider how one's capacity to love and be loved comes about.

During ontogenetic development, many seductive moments with both mother and father interact with a child's "innocent" sexuality. The child's sexuality is implanted through the medium of his or her parent's sexuality. For example, the little girl who, in a completely innocent way, is invited by her father to join him in his taking a shower will develop a different image of herself than that of a little girl whose father (and possibly her mother, too) constantly hides his or her body from her as if there were something both mysterious and possibly even sinful going on.

So what does sex represent for the adult? Lear (1991) suggests that "human sexuality is an incarnation of love, a force for unification present wherever there is life" (p.147). But he does not tell us, as we have been seeing as the views of so many in this investigation, that the happiness of romantic coupling is at best only transient and cannot last. Psychoanalysts have informed us that sexual gratification may not cement a relationship, but, instead, may mobilize its destruction by stimulating envy, jealousy and hate. Of course the myths of the media in our consumerist culture suggest differently. We are told that if we possess a beautiful body we will achieve salvation from unhappiness. The subtext is that good sex is more valuable than all the riches of the world. Naturally, then, we find men sexually interested but not committed and women complaining that, though sexually interested, they are unable to find men willing to commit to long term relationships with an eye to building a family. Such narcissistic men, though, are put off by women not in step with their fantasy of sexual conquest and the idea of love as trophy. Yet many women find more sweet and genuine men unattractive as they fail to live up to their own narcissistic need for a hero or an older, successful type. Then there is the frustration and potential embarrassment of dating and facing likely rejection in the shopping mall environment of interchangeable product. Some of this has been overcome with the advent of internet dating and the relative anonymity of cyber-space. Sex can now be ordered on line and is as potentially playful and casual as virtual reality can provide. In some ways this development has been beneficial as it has reduced the risks of embarrassment and rejection while enhancing the possibility to "hook up" sexually. It is also recognized as a prerogative of both sexes quite apart from the question of commitment and marriage: a "virtual" natural right as it were.

Indeed, as women today often describe themselves as being lonely, curious and "horny," they are not constrained from looking for arousal and gratification outside the cage of marriage. In this, they have become the equal of men who unashamedly seek sexual gratification for its own sake. Although the hook-ups offered by the many and various dating services do result in an occasional couple's getting married, more often the allure of such services lies in the promise of quick, uncomplicated sex in all forms. For example, there is a network that describes varied offerings of sado-masochism sexual engagement ranging from psychological play to physical play and the application of pain. One can choose rather as one might choose from a varied dinner menu for whatever delectable choice that seems to wet the appetite on a given night. Men and women who have been unable to attract sexual partners for a variety of reasons may now unashamedly communicate with another interested partner, see his or her picture and become an e-mail correspondent possibly leading to a date or sex. Indeed, some men seeking submissive partners have been satisfied by women seeking dominant males (and vice versa) in partners trained by the other in the course of repeated e-mail "encounters." Of course, there are always possible scenarios of disillusion and disconnect as when, for example, sado-masochistic play crosses the boundary of tolerable infliction of pain and one of the parties to it withdraws; or when emotional attachment conflicts with the implications of the sexual role playing of domineering/dominated, etc.

Possible gains for women in this new found equality in competing with men in the market place for sexual gratifications of all kinds has allowed the freeing in them of more aggressive trends. Indeed, no longer do women have to be constrained by the reaction formation implicit in playing out the role of the world's most sweet, charming, feminine hostess. Women can be as outspoken as men. As early as 1953, Ditzion wrote that the single standard defining acceptable sexual roles was a "male" standard that, allowing men to be at one with their sexuality, enabled them to feel free of the accusation of "hypersexuality." Meanwhile, it allowed women some relief from the constraints placed upon them by the more rigid sexual mores arising out of more traditional aspects of family and culture. Today, then, women, like their male counterparts, have the option of using the internet to find either casual hookups or, as in the case of their male counterparts, to seek more long term connections.

In today's world, however, erotic experiences are not limited to the outspoken cyber sex scene. In big cities like New York, men and women can enjoy an erotic experience simply by walking down the street, acknowledging and exchanging flirtatious looks from one another as they pass by in a tide of libidinal energy. Yet the internet is also a place for married men and women to seek extramarital pleasures. Gay men and women use it for the same purposes acknowledging the relative safety that cyber-space offers them in comparison to the days where the only alternative was to pick up a complete stranger off the street. Thus the impersonality of cyber-space offers both greater safety and more access to a possible date and sexual encounter than was the case when such meetings were mediated by potentially more intruding social circumstances. One can make choices by simply viewing a picture and description of a possible date and learn more in the safety of e-mail exchanges before meeting. Thus the internet provides a way to overcome hurt and disappointment from past love relationships or as a way to overcome the restricting effects of shyness.

Palac, (1998) in his book The Edge of the Bed overhears three women talking to each other. The first one complains that she is tired of sex. Passion, lust and burning desire are tiring after a while In a certain sense some of the words may sound poetic but they don't reveal the pain. Another woman had another take on it. She found out how to masturbate to orgasm by looking at porn and entertaining fantasies. Her knowledge that such fantasies are powerful and that sexual satisfaction was a state of mind that was independent of a lover satisfied her. Yet another woman describes how she used the internet to play with fantasies of dominance and submission and was turned on erotically. But then she wondered why pain and humiliation- the antithesis of love-could arouse her just as much as 'warm, fuzzy fantasies' about making love. In retrospect, she felt it to be a risky business.

CULTURE, GENDER AND THE CRITIQUE OF PATRIARCHY

Carol Gilligan (2003), a well known feminist psychologist and gifted writer believes, like many others, including this author, that we must recover some of the spontaneity and innocence of childhood if our love as adults is to be vivifying, engaging and pleasurable. Saying this, however, is not, thereby, to advocate impulsivity or refuge in love addictions. Rather, we refer to the early developmental stages of life described so well by Loewald (1979) where, open to the world, we find the world an open-textured and connecting experience where we are both open to the world and with ourselves in the world, a notion reminiscent of some of the existentialist ideas discussed in Chapter One in the section on Binswanger where he referred to the experiential world of Heidegger's "Dasein-analytics".

However, whereas many of us see complexities making us cautious in approaching the issue of how we can better love in this sense more "naturally" and spontaneously within or without the context of current cultural restrictions, Gilligan fearlessly sets out to "take the bull by the horns"! She insists that ancient patriarchal culture is to blame for the dichotomies and splits in our psyches first classified and elaborated in a "scientific" way by Freud when he introduced his developmental account of psychic realization centered about his now-famous concept of the Oedipus complex. In a word, she identifies the concept of the Oedipus complex itself as part of the problem. Instead of a natural law of psychic organization and development, as it were, she sees it, rather, as a socio-historical ideological construction reflecting the continuing socio-cultural bias of patriarchy in our times. Thus, without knowing it, it seems, psychoanalysis has unwittingly been complicit in reproducing patriarchy by insisting upon inscribing its theory of psychic health and development within the confines of patriarchal, Oedipal dynamics; insisting, that is, that psychic health and happiness requires the attainment of post-Oedipal, developmental organization.

As a replacement for this patriarchal ordering of the psyche by the Oedipus complex, she introduces the myth of Cupid and Psyche believing that this fable will help shed light upon a less restricting paradigm for psychic organization and happiness; one that, by undoing the repressing strategies underlying the construction of gender roles as currently ordained under patriarchy and ratified by the Oedipal psychology of traditional psychoanalytic theory, will permit a greater degree of pleasure in our lives. Her book, *The Birth of Pleasure,* outlines this seductive alternative.

Now, of course, to notice that there are certain restrictions inherent in patriarchy is not new. Anthropologists, analysts and philosophers have been discussing these issues for many years. In fact, much of what is now known as post-structuralist philosophy takes, as its point of departure, precisely this question. Nor is Gilligan's position necessarily a particularly radical alternative to the way the construction of gender is sometimes understood within a patriarchal, socio-cultural context. Indeed, in many ways she offers a quite moderate, and beautifully expressed, alternative frame for reconsidering the way so-called masculine and feminine identifications within each of the sexes needs to be reconfigured in order to oppose some the repressive effects of patriarchy that she sees as ratified by the structural idea (myth) of the Oedipus.

Gilligan is not, however, motivated to be gratuitously engaged in Freud-bashing. In fact, she sees him as having in many ways empowered the forces at odds with the forces of patriarchal repression if only by having so clearly identified their inner workings. She also gives Freud credit for having empowered his female patients by trying as hard to understand them and in the same fashion as he tried to understand his male patients. But, to the extent that he is a force in the continuation of the dominion of patriarchy in the pejorative sense she always seems to mean by that term, she *is* critical:

> It is a hierarchy or priesthood in which a father or some fathers control access to truth or power or God or knowledge to salvation in whatever form it takes. As such, patriarchy is an order of domination, privileging some men over others and subordinating women (p. 7).

In her eloquent description, she points out how patriarchy in this pejorative sense establishes hierarchies in the heart of intimacy and, by wreaking havoc with innocence, creates trauma and so is inherently *tragic*. It represses the voices of innocence in each of us, and, instead, colonizes the psyche with an externally imposed agenda of pre-ordained and, therefore, un-spontaneous behaviors furthering the laws and rituals of a patriarchal order—as though such were, as it were, pre-ordained *fate*. So, too, for example, she sees the concept of destiny, separation and other ancient dicta equated with "freedom" as interdicting a more authentic expression (or voice) of soul and psyche. The moral she extracts from the myth of Psyche and Cupid, her alternative to the patriarchal myth of the Oedipus, is that when patriarchal laws are broken, when the difficult task of rejoining our genuine love feelings is, through difficult labors, accomplished, then the result is pleasure, spontaneity, authenticity and a greater measure of innocence.

We need to look more closely, however, at what Gilligan means by 'pleasure' and 'love'. To begin, she defines the self and soul as a 'core consciousness' which is also rooted in the body. Pleasure is first and foremost a bodily sensation the feeling of which is experienced as the emotion of delight and joy. It is the secret well-spring of our minds and hearts that transforms us beyond our mere life histories, genetic make-up and culture. It allows us to *know* the truth, not merely as a dissociated intellectual matter, but as knowledge of a felt-experience that knits us deeply with our in-most, affective core. Freeing love means to release it and allow it to arrange into its own, natural psychic patterns.

It is the nature of love as freedom, to choose and not be bound by the rituals of patriarchy including the Oedipus drama. Thus, as Psyche walks out of this patterning and breaks the prohibitions of patriarchy, she walks out of the Oedipus myth and refuses to sacrifice herself and her children for the sake of immortality. Her love of Cupid is now openly recognized and the latter, in an appeal to his father, Jupiter, is granted a happy marriage and immortality.

What, one may ask, does Gilligan make of Cupid's appeal to his father in order to gain permission for his happiness, and legitimacy for his marriage? Is not the inherent (or latent) truth of the myth rather that Psyche must first deal with Venus' antagonism (the mother) in order to resolve competitive impulses; and only then appeal, through Cupid, to the other half (the father) before a happy ending can be assured?

What, then, of 'love'? Gilligan agrees that love driven merely by emotion may be blind. It can also be silent. How, then, is it to prevail? How is it to get from the locked world of the one-person world of patriarchy to the two-person world of relatedness. Unrequited love—so much the quality of the one-person world under patriarchy (in her sense)—is bound to be tragic as it cannot be publicly recognized, reciprocated in the other and, thus, find its fulfillment. It is a love suffered in silence. On this analysis, it follows that 'love' and 'relatedness', though different things, are both necessary if there is to be 'love' that is fulfilled (requited).

There are also differences between 'love' in this sense and 'relationships'. Being in a relationship does not guarantee its being one of fulfillment in Gilligan's sense of 'love', above. Moreover, constraints upon the feelings of joy and pleasure that degrade love do so for both men and women equally. Love in Gilligan's sense is not just about finding any partner, for it is as much about finding a part of one's-self as it is in finding another; but it depends upon finding a reciprocating and open heart in the other, one in touch with his or her "pleasure" as well, if there is to be fulfillment in love. When cut off from the pleasure of love, the self, according to Gilligan, erects a protective wall around itself insulating it from intimacy. Thus, there can be no intimacy without relatedness in the sense that Gilligan describes above.

In Gilligan's mind, dissociation is the enemy of pleasure and love. The defensive dissociative mechanisms between image and memory, between the look of things and the way things feel, contain two different worlds: what you feel and what you really feel; the story you tell yourself about what happened and what really happened; the experience and the way it must be re-contextualized in order to fit the categories of patriarchy. Love, in Gilligan's sense, must be freely given and enjoyed by two. Again, if love is not to be *tragic,* it must be inscribed in a two-person world: one face, one voice and two persons, ". . . an epiphany, a moment of sudden radical illumination" (p. 213).

Relating her own work with patients with the work of infant research, Gilligan points out it has been found that, in our current culture, boys begin to take on the masculine roles of patriarchy in her pejorative sense at about the age of five and lose their joyous gestures of love for their other boy friends, for example, and, instead, become more driven to become "little men of patriarchy", wooden and aggressive, obsessed with games about "good" guys versus "bad" guys. Girls, on the other hand, she says, take on the roles of "the feminine" in our culture later, in early adolescence, and are more likely to see it as a role they are compelled to play, becoming more self-conscious about what they are doing and how they appear. In both cases, there is a loss of spontaneity, a loss of pleasure and, consequently, a loss of love.

Under patriarchy, the mother-son son relationship requires that the mother sacrifice her relationship with her son or the initiation rites of masculinity cannot go forward. If she refuses, the fear (and prohibition) is that her son will experience the world through his mother's eyes. Thus, little boys must disavow their "feminine" identifications. Likewise, under patriarchy in this sense, pleasure is the hallmark of a "bad" woman if she is too connected with her sexuality. She is seen as curious, "fallen" and irrelevant to the game of getting her "man", a process more of acquiescence to submission than a free spontaneous realization of love. By, once again, relying upon the myth of Psyche and Cupid, Gilligan is able to illustrate the difference between a loving woman (free, spontaneous love), and the loving of the dissociated image of a woman under patriarchy.

For Gilligan, like Jessica Benjamin (1995), who in many ways makes similar points, it is the Oedipalization, as it were, of identity that results in stripping it of what Benjamin terms "identificatory love". By identificatory love, Benjamin means that which is part of pre-oedipal identity that, not surprisingly, involves large measures of identification by each sex with the parent of the opposite sex. Thus, little boys feel maternal feelings for their male peers while little girls feel masculine (or phallic) interest for their female peers and, as adults, both feel ways characteristic of the opposite sex towards one another. According to Benjamin, if this aspect of identity is not carried through, into and out of, the Oedipal phase of development, relationships devolve into one-dimensional rituals of domination and submission, at the cost of "subject-ness" (what Gilligan would call 'pleasure') for each partner.

But what of the fact, mentioned already, that, according to the Cupid and Psyche myth, when Psyche flees, Cupid loves her all the more and begs his

father's intervention to allow the transgression of the Oedipal tragedy (patriarchy) so that he might realize his love. Gilligan explains:

> Jupiter acts to remove the ligaments of patriarchy, making their relationship no
> longer uneven and freeing their love from the threat that Cupid must leave Psy-
> che if she does not obey him (p. 157).

But, again, isn't it a seeming contradiction to Gilligan's argument that the
non-tragic (i.e. non-Oedipal) outcome the Cupid Psyche myth is supposed to
illustrate, depends upon Jupiter's (i.e., Cupid's father's) intervention. A possible rebuttal might be, perhaps, that it takes a father to undo *the patriarchal
order of the Father* by ratifying a new order and then, voluntarily, desisting in
furthering the old order as ordained by the previous form of his law—rather,
perhaps, as George Washington abdicated the role of kingship in favor of in-
stituting a new, less hierarchal constitution permitting greater equality
amongst men. Gilligan does not speculate upon this possibility as she seems
not to notice this apparent problem.

One thing she is clear about, however, is that by loosening the effects of the
Oedipal complex upon what is considered masculine and what is considered
feminine (that is, by allowing identificatory love), there will abound an effu-
sion of polymorphous pleasure, hence, "spontaneity" in the 'love' of both
men and women. Again, it is the rigidities of the Oedipal order, the imposi-
tion of a one-dimensional gender dichotomy between "male" and "female",
that imposes such sacrifices upon ourselves that we suffer a loss of spontaneity in our capacity to love. So, for example, masculinity, under patriarchy,
seems to require standing alone and forgoing the sweetness of relationships
of polymorphous pleasure in relating both masculine and feminine aspects
of identity; while femininity, under patriarchy, seems to require loss of female phallic spontaneity for masochistic submission creating, dare we say,
"Stepford"-like syndromes of anomie in the way women must relate to the
men of patriarchy. Both of these outcomes have tragic endings by denying
vulnerability, tenderness, intimacy and "pleasure". No proper 'love' relationship can thrive in such a desert:

> When parents are bound to uphold idealized images of mothers and fathers, thus
> concealing parts of themselves; when a boy's expression of tenderness and vul-
> nerability arouse fears about his ability to be a man—it interferes in a confiding
> relationship, just as concerns about femininity stand in the way of girls speak-
> ing freely (p. 30).

Throughout, Gilligan turns to the modality of couple's counseling as a lab-
oratory to make her case. She finds that trust is created by the following pre-

cepts: (a) I will never leave you; (b) I will never lie to you; (c) I will never try to possess you. As she says, both love and democracy depend upon having a voice and a returning resonance that comes from being able to speak and be heard. She concludes:

> Nothing is what it appears to be, but everything is exactly what it is. There are no secrets. It is the art, then, of circumlocution of learning to approach the truth from many sides (p. 231).

Indeed, a fine trope by which to end; for is not the principle of pluralism most apt in expressing her wish to rekindle a more polymorphous pleasure from within the confines of, in her mind, the otherwise more one-dimensional "Oedipalization" of psychic experience under patriarchy?

In response, however, it seems fair to ask whether, in retrospect, she might have over-stated her case somewhat. For example, in our discussion in Chapter Six of male and female psycho-sexual development in relation to love and loving, it may be recalled that Hamon (2000), Diamond (2004) and Ross (2000) all contribute to the development of what might be considered a competing account to Gilligan's insistence that the only appropriate solution to repressive gender roles is the overthrow of the Oedipus myth. Indeed, all three of these opposing authors, in their various ways, seem to point to the possibility for a non-repressive Oedipal order where each gender is able to carry through the Oedipal threshold precisely those aspects of identification with the opposite sex that Gilligan and Benjamin are concerned in safeguarding; namely, those that allow for a more varied dialectic of interrelating complementary gender aspects in the sexual interaction of each party to a couple in their love relation to each other.

The possibility of such a competing account to Gilligan's, then, suggests, perhaps, a too hasty re-drawing of psychoanalytic wisdom by the discarding of the Oedipal myth altogether. Surely, as theorists of our clinical observations, we need to be careful not to create theoretical models that, in an effort to bring to the attention of interested clinicians and theorists important ideas alleviating unnecessary suffering, over-hastily discard well established structural ideas important in capturing aspects of the very complex dynamics underlying mature psychic health and happiness. That is, in our shared zest to reform the theory and practice of psychoanalysis in order to reflect a continuing openness to better understand the conditions permitting greater happiness in love and deeper integration in work, we must be on guard not to throw the baby out with the bath water. In this regard, Carroll Gilligan has created a beautifully argued and provocative challenge to precisely this question of the validity of psychoanalytic self-understanding as it exists currently in both theory and practice; one that requires close attention and careful consideration.

REFERENCES

Benda, C.E. (1961) *The Image of Love.* Chicago: Free Press.

Benjamin, J. (1995) *Like Subjects, Love Objects, Essays on Recognition and Sexual Difference.* New Haven: Yale University Press.

Campbell, J. (1988) *The Power of Myth.* New York: Doubleday.

Diamond, M.J. (2004) Assessing the multiple within: a psychoanalytic perspective on the transformation of masculinity at mid-life. *International Journal of Psychoanalysis, 85:*45–64.

Diztion, S. (1953) *Marriage, Morals and Sex in America.* New York: Bookman Assoc.

Drassinower, A. (2003) *Freud's Theory of Culture: Eros, Loss and Politics.* Lanham, MD: Towman & Littlefield.

Fenichel, O. (1945) *The Psychoanalytic Theory of Neurosis.* New York: Norton.

Freud, S. (1913) On transience. *S.E., 14:*303–307.

———. (1930) Civilization and its discontents. *S.E., 21:*57–145.

Gargiulo, G. (1987) Superman heroes and the American ego-ideal. *Issues in Ego Psychology, 10*: 59–64.

Gilligan, C. (2003) *The Birth of Pleasure—A New Map of Love.* New York: Vintage Books.

Gordon, L. (1969) Beyond the reality principle: illusion or reality? IPTAR newsletter, 1969.

Hamon, M.C. (2000) *Why Do Women Love Men and Not Their Mothers?* New York: The Other Press.

Lear, J. (1991) *Love and Its Place in Nature.* New York: Noonday.

Loewald, H.W. (1951) Ego and reality. In: *The Essential Loewald.* (ed) Jonathan Lear, Hagerstown: University Publishing Group, 2000.

Palac, L. (1998) *The Edge of the Bed.* New York: Little Brown & Co.

Person, E.S. (2004) Personal power and the cultural unconscious: implications for psychoanalytic theories of sex and gender. *Journal of the American Academy for Psychoanalysis and Dynamic Psychiatry, 32:*59–75.

Ross, M.J. (2000) What do men want? *Issues in Psychoanalytic Psychology, 22:*53–68.

Slavin, J. (2002) The innocence of sexuality. *Psychoanalytic Quarterly, LXXI:*51–79.

Stephen, M. (2003) Male mothers and cannibal women: a Kleinian interpretation of male initiation in the New Guinea Highlands. *Psychoanalytic Review, 90:*615–635.

Chapter Eight

Commitment

LOVE, SEXUALITY AND COMMITMENT

In addressing love, sexuality and commitment we need to look once again at what goes on in the context of the relationship of "the couple." As discussed earlier, the selection of partners arising out of a prior relationship of friendship may be more fruitful and less hazardous in the long run than a selection based on merely physical characteristics like looks and sexual "chemistry." Connection through personal qualities of personality valued and enjoyed by each in relation to the other bodes much better for long term relating than connection arising out of physical attraction alone. Yet attraction through the personal characteristics enjoyed by each in relation to the other does not guarantee a long term relationship. The qualities we find attractive in a person may be counterbalanced by other traits making the prospect of a long term affair difficult and, so, less likely.

For example, a conservative young man falls in love with an attractive and intelligent divorcee with two children from her previous marriage. Besides the physical chemistry, he admires her work ethic that, similar to his own, reminds him of his own family background. Yet, perhaps he does not know that her relation to her family background is quite different in that she had rebelled against it. To his growing dismay, he finds that their political and cultural opinions are often at logger heads and he finds it difficult to tolerate the way she had brought up her children who, he feels, show no respect to others. Their coupling may largely have been as compelling as it was because of physical attraction. Yet, now, with his discovery that she is repulsed by his chauvinist and sexist attitudes, the couple have to cope with her desire for her own equal rights in the relationship, her rebellion against her family and the sense of rebellion for equal rights she had transmitted to her children. Now, given such a scenario, it seems exceedingly doubtful that such a relationship could last even with a shared work ethic as common ground between the two.

In other instances, it is more obvious early on that partnering is going to be too fraught with discord to be successful. If a man really does not want to get married but is infatuated with the beauty of a beautiful, sexy woman who enjoys her seductiveness but is not on an equal footing in the relationship in other respects and, because of such inequalities, becomes dependent upon him and wants marriage in order to feel secure, the relationship will break up fairly quickly. Even if her wish for marriage was not even verbalized, nonetheless, her vulnerability for dependent and controlling behavior might very well create a climate of mutual aggression in the form of attacks and mutual recriminations that would all too quickly leave the relationship in shambles.

In general, it remains a very difficult business to prognosticate whether a relationship will last or not quite apart from the issue of the quality of the couple's interaction. There are so many variables both seen and unseen that can make a difference. So what is the "chemistry" factor people are always talking about? People are always saying things like: "there was such marvelous chemistry, but things just seem not to have worked out. . . ." or, "No sense pursuing that, 'there's just no chemistry.'" The bottom line is that relationships last when they are comfortable for both partners. Infatuations and the early onset of passion and ardor in a beginning relationship may start with fire but end in explosion and break-up. Dynamics in a relationship often pull in two different directions, towards symbiosis on the one hand while, on the other, towards individuation and the need for self-realization. The couple's playground may become a battle ground for the two families of origin as they try to jockey for position in a battle to see which will be most influential in directing the lives of the hapless couple.

But we stray from our discussion on the question of "chemistry." What causes attraction? Prof. Pines (1999) of Ben Gurion University in Israel believes that the sense of familiarity is central. We look for familiar faces or features that remind us of our families. While we seek partners who are similar, opposites also attract each other for different reasons. Men want the woman to look good, to be shorter than they are, to be successful, kind, easy to talk to and of roughly their same age. Women, on the other hand, look for men who are taller than they are, independent and kind, easy to talk to and older than they are. While men emphasize sexual attraction as a key factor in choosing a partner, women often emphasize the quality of the relationship as upper most in their consideration for a partner. Most people look for someone who is neither more nor less attractive than they are. While sexual purity is no longer required, trustworthiness and emotional stability still top the list as upper-most in the minds of individuals seeking partners.

No matter what the rationalization, though, as long as idealization by each partner of the other lasts, the partners of such idealizations tend to stick together. But unconscious forces often play an ever greater role in the dynamics of a couple than the surface rationalizations made by each party in his or her own conscious minds. We often look for someone with the same level of maturity or someone who suffered a similar psychological injury (in need of healing) as suffered by one's self. The most frequent causes for falling in love, though, are (a) the beloved provides something that the lover needs or, (b) there is a sense of being valued in return. Most importantly, then, if we want to live a life of love, we must be open to loving and we must find a partner who is similarly open to loving in return.

The latest research on selecting mates informs that people are attracted to others whom they perceive as secure, similar to themselves and similar, in their ideal selves, to one and other's ideals; for a sense of security is found in familiarity and security is linked to well-being and a sense of the capacity to survive. A study of 751 college students at the University of Iowa evaluated potential partners with two different attachment styles: secure partners who are supportive and confident in their relationships, and insecure partners who are preoccupied, fearful and dismissing in their relationships. Less secure romantic partners often with anxiety centered around fears of abandonment, tend to avoid expressing emotions in a relationship. But regardless of the participant's own attachment style, the study showed that people are most attracted to secure romantic partners. When it comes to attraction to insecurely attached partners, participants tend to be attracted to those who are similar to themselves. Again, we are reminded that when in love we are often swept up by an ardor that clouds more reality oriented based decisions, making more considered choices difficult at best. Attraction is as much a construction of the lover as it is about who the beloved, in some sense, "really" is. Indeed, is not beauty in the eye of the beholder!

Varied sexual and relational roles for couples have been described by Kernberg (1995) in great detail. We find, for example, that in masochistic characters, excessive pain is transformed into aggression. Such aggression, in turn, distorts and undoes psychic structures necessary to bind the aggression resulting in its expression in the acting out of impulsive behavior rather than being contained in fantasy. In erotic masochism, sexual excitement is experienced through the wish to be humiliated in the total submission to a partner. Some women with depressive masochistic characters will fall in love with unavailable men leading to romantic encounters in unrealistic situations or to romantic fantasies of what "might have been." Fixation to an original trauma of unrequited love creates a seemingly endless need to repeat the same experience. Even worse, the unrequited nature of the love tends to increase the ardor of the hopeless love rather than diminish it.

On the other hand, Kernberg (1995) is also interested in discussing narcissistic personalities in his discussion of 'love.' Typically, in such persons, an idealized partner becomes an appendix or satellite to the narcissist where, in the unconscious, each is a reflection replicating the other. Such individuals cannot accept their partner's dependency needs and fear being exploited or transgressed against. They experience the ordinary back and forth in human relations as exploitative and invasive:

> Because of conflicts around unconscious envy, they cannot experience gratitude
> for what they receive from the other, whose very capacity to give freely they
> may envy. Their lack of gratitude precludes the strengthening of the capacity for
> loving appreciation of love received (p.151).

ATTACHMENT STYLES

Fonagy (2003) stresses that human attachment propels cognitive development. Close proximity to caregivers is a necessary condition for the proper development of the capacity to connect. Disruption of early loving attachments undermines capabilities vital to social development. Already at the age of three months, the infant develops ideas about the external world from the mirroring and facial responses of the caregiver. If parental mirroring is in sync with the child's need and is read accurately by the child, these parental cues become signals that contribute to the child's self-regulation of affect. If out of sync, or read inaccurately, parental interactions appear to escalate the disruptive effects of affect in the child rather than modulating them. The latter mode, if prevailing, leads the child to experience the world in a distorted and disjointed way. There is activated in the insufficiently mirrored child, the need to develop manipulative and controlling strategies in which the attachment figure is required to perform rescue functions to rid the self of unbearable internal representations.

When we speak of 'attachment', we cannot help but speak about processes that make such bonds possible. A symbolic system is needed for mental states and to be able to activate selective states of mind in line with particular intentions. Disruption of early affectionate bonds sets up maladaptive attachment patterns and limits social development. Babies differentiate physiological stimuli that accompany different emotions through observing their mother's facial responses. A second order representational symbolic system is formed for his mental states. If met with the caregiver's reciprocity it helps with self-regulation. If it is met inaccurately or even ignored it will escalate affect rather than modulate it.

Mentalization is the capacity to think about affects as separate from causing action and represents a developmental achievement—the integration of pretend modes of thinking and their psychic equivalent modes of functioning (play). However, hyperarousal and failure of mentalization go hand in hand. When projective identification is utilized, individuals cannot experience themselves from within; rather, they experience self through enactments without. Failure of mentalization leads to breakdown in identity and the emergence of dissociation. Thinking is concrete and 'love' as a concept or symbol is available only as physical experience.

People living with each other develop special sensitivities to one another for better or for worse. They bring to the coupling process their own individual attachment styles and, through the prism of such reality filtering, become exquisitely attuned to their partner's strengths and weaknesses. Emotional reactions produce bodily reactions which, in turn, activate affect. Posture, eye contact and the use of words may lead to physical arousal. Researchers Goldstein & Thau (2004) have found that degree of arousal of the husband's nervous system is the best predictor of unhappiness for both partners. Couples regulate their internal affective response to their relationships by balancing out perceived positive to negative events in the quality of their relatedness at a ratio of five to one. Among couples who split, 10 out of every 100 comments were perceived as insults. In order to lower the temperature of a fight, couples might use words of "repair." Those who can't use regulatory words, keep frozen in a combat posture. During fights, hearts beat faster, blood pressure climbs, the stomach constricts and stress hormones course through the body. Under circumstances of high arousal, attempts at communication remain futile. Men hit the boiling point more rapidly, are more vulnerable to such extremes, tend to remain aroused and often channel such arousal by obsession for revenge.

Couples who stay together have mastered techniques of soothing each other and are able to prevent undue distress to one another during times of conflict. Certain transition phases in life such as parenthood, tend to produce an enormous amount of stress to a couple. Extra-marital affairs can provide another shock, often devastating, to the couple's system. Oddly enough, the straying partner is usually as satisfied with his marital love life as is the partner who does not stray. Meanwhile, those couples who stay together report that, for the most part, their lives have been more enriched than not by their staying together, even when there is conflict. With the advent of aging, marital differences are less subject to erupt into fighting. And with age, gender differences seem to fade away, and are often replaced by a more unified view of marriage and life.

The more effective a couple is in regulating affects within the system, the longer lasting is the relationship. This can be achieved by increasing the sense of security of the couple. Thus in couples' therapy, for example, the focus of treatment shifts from the security of the individual to the security of the couple. Attachment schemas are formed out of the quality of early systems of relatedness and become non-conscious procedural (or formal) memories that are later evoked in other interpersonal experience. These attachment dynamics, operating outside awareness, come into play in the regulation of affect within the dyadic relatedness of a couple. When such schema are seriously challenged or the bond is compromised, couples either seek treatment or go their separate ways with all the disruption of soul and heartbreak associated thereto. Affects of fear and shame replace confidence and trust. In treatment, couples learn to accept the hard fact that dissention and fights are part of love. They learn to tolerate moments of mis-attunement associated not only with the effect of harsh words from one another, but from the corrosive effects of silence masking anger and fear. Such silences, pregnant with underlying anger, may be experienced by a partner as dismissive and degrading repetitions enacting earlier still active "toxic" attachment schemas from earlier relationships with primary objects of "care."

Bergmann (2000) has focused on thinking dysfunctional couples in terms of the concept of a couple's "mutual neurosis." He cites Freud's preconditions for "being in love," and reminds us that by these standards it is no wonder that coupling is, inevitably, an act of relatedness through "complementary neurosis." In an effort to avoid the dynamics of their parent's marriage, couples all too soon discover that, contrary to conscious wish, they are, nonetheless, caught in the rip current of repetition compulsion. Adding his voice to the fray, Kernberg (1995), distinguishes between sexual excitement, erotic desire and mature sexual love in terms of instinctual forces. He believes that there is a perverse core in all of us based on primal scene experience that results in combining competing wishes to triumph over the Oedipal parent with the wish to be sexually involved with both parents at the same time. The degree of integration of the underlying dynamics resulting from these powerful wishes determines our love and sexual destiny. Bergmann, on the other hand, believes that no matter what degree of integration, infantile needs remain forever powerful and are tempered only by the development of concern for the other.

Concern for the other appears to be the magical ingredient that cements a successful relationship allowing it to last through the ups and downs of the effects of conflict and defense in the context of instinct generated turmoil. Such "concern" is not a given or inborn quality, nor is it a product, necessarily, of infatuation or sexual attraction. Once the initial thralldom wanes and partners are faced with the illusion shattering problems of everyday life, differences between partners begin to assert themselves. Often it is small differences in habits that set partners off on a downward spiral of annoyance and irritation that can lead to more disorganizing feelings of hostility and recrimination. Who in a love relationship has never felt: "If he/she really loved me, he/she would see my point (think like me) and feel as I do, or, at least understand how I feel." In such deteriorating circumstances partners begin to suspect one another's love and concern for each other's welfare. Rainer Maria Rilke (1982), in *Letters to a Young Poet*, recognized the dilemma.

While it is good to love, it is also very difficult. Love between two people is the most difficult task and perhaps the final proof that culminates and is the end of many other labors and tasks that went before. Young people are not prepared to love, they need to learn it. But we learn from self reflection and thus such time is a long and secluded time. For a long time, loving is lonely and experienced in solitude.

Rilke seems to be reminding us that, in the face of stormy disagreement and misunderstanding, though we may have doubt about whether our partner truly loves us, nonetheless, in the end, we can repair the connection and reaffirm our love. Yet, love is not for the weak of heart; for only the bravest win out in the end. The insight that love must be willingly learned before being mastered is well expressed in the following passage by Jane Lahr and Lena Tabori (1982) in the Forward to *Love: A Celebration of Art & Literature*:

> True love is reciprocal, is neither a difficult or mysterious emotion. Love is the act of extending oneself to nurture another. It takes a conscious act of will to learn to love. Love is a discipline (p. 13).

The difference between Rilke and the above may well reflect two different persons with different backgrounds. Rilke was a disappointed romantic poet for whom peace eluded him. Lahr and Tabori, on the other hand, unlike Rilke, proclaim that love is not difficult if hearts are open to it. From a psychoanalytic perspective we might rather say that if one has grown up with love from the beginning with the love of loving parents, the way to love is open whereas, where parental loving was deficient or distorted through parental discord and mis-attunement, one may find the doors to love difficult to open. Where we felt humiliated and hurt, we will look for unrealistic compensations and choose a partner narcissistically. Such a person will experience great difficulty in being able to recognize the subjectivity of the other as separate yet still loving. Such anathema is, perhaps, best considered in conclusion of this chapter with these wise words of Martin Buber.

Buber said while there are many feelings in a man, man is content to dwell in his love. Love cannot be selfish and view the loved one as a possession. Love is between two people, two selves. Love is the responsibility for the other.

REFERENCES

Bergmann, M. (2000) Mutual neurosis and the revival of sexuality in the life of the couple. *Issues in Psychoanalytic Psychology, 22:*5–19.

Buber, M. I and Thou. In: *Love: A Celebration of Art & Literature,* (ed.) Jane Lahr and Lena Tabori, p. 224. New York: Stewart, Tabori & Chaing Publishers, 1982.

Fonagy, P, M. Target, G. Gergeley, J. Allen & A, Bateman (2003). The developmental roots of borderline personality disorder in early attachment relationships: a theory and some evidence. *Psychoanalytic Inquiry, 23:*412–459.

Goldstein, S. & S. Thau.(2004) Attachment theory, neuroscience, and couple therapy. *Psychologist/Psychoanalyst, 24:*15–19.

Kernberg, O. (1995) *Love Relations: Normality and Pathology.* New Haven: Yale U. Press.

Lahr, J. & Lena Tabori (1982) (Eds.) *Love: A Celebration in Art and Literature.* New York: Stewart, Tabori & Chaing Publishers.

Pines, A.M. (1999) *Falling in Love. Why We Choose the Lovers We Choose.* London: Routledge.

Rilke, R. M. Letters to a young poet. In: *Love: A Celebration of Art & Literature,* (ed.) Jane Lahr and Lena Tabori, p. 205. New York: Stewart, Tabori & Chaing Publishers, 1982.

Chapter Nine

Love in Psychoanalysis

CRITIQUE OF PSYCHOANALYTIC THEORY

Early on Norman O. Brown (1959) criticized psychoanalytic theory as being too rational, as being too much influenced by economic materialism and neglecting the spiritual dimension of human hopes and desires. In his book *Life Against Death*, he credits Freud with opening up new possibilities for understanding human nature but laments that since his death his theories have become a closed scholastic system ". . . itself no exception to the general cultural trend toward stereotype and sterility" (p. xii). In his opinion, the whole meta-psychological superstructure needs reinterpretation to fit into a wider general theory of human nature, culture and history: to become a new stage for man to know himself. To him, it appears that Freud's theory is based upon a concept of repression and man's refusal to recognize the realities of human nature. This is contrasted to ". . . Man's [need to] hold fast to the deep rooted, passionate strivings for a positive fulfillment in happiness" (p. 8).

Brown believes that the link between the theory of neurosis and history is the theory of religion. Neurotic symptoms contain truths; they are expressions of the "immortal desires of the human heart". Psychoanalysis, then, must concern itself with the mysteries of the heart (or soul); and religion is the heart of that mystery. Naturally enough, Brown refers to the importance of love in Christianity. The Jewish religion, although as much concerned with these issues, is perhaps more resonant with the idea advanced by Schweitzer (1964) of 'the reverence for life'. For example, a rabbinical interpretation for God's anger at Moses and Aron in spite of Moses' following through with God's instruction to strike a rock so as to provide his people with water, is banishment from seeing the Holy Land. It turns out that his harsh punishment was due to

Moses' failure to have sufficiently mourned the death of his sister Miriam. Her grave was near the rock that provided the water and it was expected that both Moses and Aron would commemorate Miriam during the carrying out of God's instructions at the rock.

And again, for Brown, "[t]he riddle of history is not Reason (Freud) but Desire; not labor, but love" (p 16). Freud assumed that work and economic necessity were the essence of the reality principle; but the essence of Man, for Brown, is repressed desire. It is and always will be the energy necessary for the labor to make history. Repressed Eros is the force of history and labor is its sublimated form:

> Psychoanalytic consciousness, as a higher stage in the general consciousness of mankind, maybe likewise the fulfillment of the historical consciousness, that ever widening and deepening search for origins which has obsessed Western thought since the renaissance (p. 19).

As we know, the aim of Eros is union with objects outside the self, but, importantly, it is also the force that enlivens the self with narcissistic effusions of self-loving. Narcissistic desire is the seeking of pleasure in the activity of one's own body. The pattern for all human love is based upon the primal narcissistic experience of union of the self with a world of pleasure and love.

According to Brown, another problem with psychoanalysis is that it lacks a general theory of art. He sees this as following from the fact that Freud privileges the reality principle over and above the pleasure principle. Brown argues that it is Man's desire to change reality to conform to the pleasure principle that is the driving force underlying all creativity and art. Moreover, this driving force, according to Brown, is the motivation underlying all life. Because it is the goal or telos of Man it also expresses an appropriate Weltanschauung. Even Freud, cited in Brown (1959), suggests that playfulness is important as it takes us back to childhood pleasures:

> Its contradiction of the reality principle is its social function, as a constant reinforcement of the struggle for instinctual liberation; its childishness is to the professional critic a stumbling block, but to the artist its glory (p. 58).

A third observation of Brown's is that psychoanalysis has no theory of language. Language, of course (he says), must originate in the early mother-dyad and therefore be a language of pleasure and love before it becomes oriented by work and the reality principle. He cites Susan Langer (1948) who, in describing how language began, says: ". . . it started as purposeless lolling-instincts, primitive aesthetic reactions and dreamlike association of ideas" (p. 70). He then cites Cassirer (1944) who addressed the metaphorical aspects

of language noting how, as words are organized by metaphor, language relates to itself in the tendency of words to play on words. As language is oriented as well by magic and the omnipotence of thought, it is not, therefore,
merely an act of descriptive representation; for it also includes the dimension
of wish:

> Language as play and language as disease are the two sides of language as wish
> fulfillment thinking, and wish fulfillment thinking is a legacy of childhood in-
> delible in our minds, carrying the secret project of the pure pleasure-ego, the
> search for an erotic sense of reality. (p.72).

Brown also rejects Freud's dual instinct theory and the repetition compulsion in favor of a theory of aggression. According to Brown, aggression is a
mixture of both Eros and Thanatos.
This duality then becomes expressed in a dialogic structuring of mind and
awareness. For example, the capacity for man to understand the fact of his own
immortality is an instance of the dialogic nature of human self-consciousness.
Other animals, lacking this quality of mind seem merely to live and die without
the capacity for this self-insight of their own condition. Unlike mankind, these
other animals do not "worry" about past or future in this sense. They lack the capacity of dialogic mindedness. For Brown, death anxiety manifests itself not as
an ontological imperative, but as an historical fact in relation to the fact of repression, in this case the repression of the human body itself. On this account,
the horror of death becomes the horror in the realization of all of the unlived possibilities, of other lives not lived, as it were, but stored up within our bodies as
potentialities now forever unrealizable. And, what of sublimation? Brown cites
Ferenczi as saying that sublimation is madness. Plato defined philosophy as sublimation; its goal to elevate mind over matter in a deepening of "the spiritual".
In contrast, Brown sees all of western philosophy as a sort of "civilized shaman-
ism"; a form of life that, driven by the quest for a higher mode of living he thinks
is especially adapted to the cosmopolitan needs of urban living. The prototype
of sublimation, he says, is to be found in infant thumb-sucking where the child
makes himself into both himself and his mother's breast at the same time. The
madness of this sublimation, however, consists in its being life that is, at the
same time, a denial of life. Its basic mechanism is negation:

> Although the world of fantasy is that opaque shield with which the ego protects
> itself from reality through which the ego sees reality; it is by living in a world
> of fantasy that we lead a desexualized life (p. 165).

He sees the possibility of overcoming repression through the dialectics of
making the unconscious conscious; a process made possible in principle by

the ego's synthesizing ability to overcome its internal splits and conflicts. It is via the force of Eros that underlies and makes possible the synthesizing mode of mind, however, that Brown thinks creates the possibility for cure and unity of our "dialectical consciousness". Moreover, Brown believes that Freud (1930), however tentatively, shared this idea and expressed as much in his *Civilization and its Discontents*:

> Man have brought their powers of subduing forces of nature to such a pitch that by using them they could now very easily exterminate one another to the last man. They know this—hence arises a great part of their current unrest, their dejection, their mood of apprehension.
>
> And now it may be expected that the other of the two "heavenly forces", eternal Eros, will put forth its strength so as to maintain himself alongside of his equally immortal adversary (p. 144).

SOLDIERS OF EROS

Martin Bergmann (1988) has taught us that, as analysts, the practitioners of psychoanalysis are "soldiers of Eros". Those having read Freud on technique, will recognize that statement as referring to the half of Freud's dual instinct theory we have been speaking about in our discussion of Norman O. Brown above. The question for Brown and, contrary to what he may have thought, for psychoanalytic practice as well, is how to create conditions for the possibility for Eros to triumph over Thanatos; how, that is, in the analytic situation, to help the patient overcome, through utilization of his transference love to the analyst, his resistance to getting better. In accomplishing this task, Freud (1915) is not sure himself about how much of this transference love should be elicited and how much received. He knew that some of his colleagues had succumbed to such love and, therefore, was more than aware of the power of love when accompanied by eroticism. Yet he stated that transference love was not all that different from ordinary love, even if, as a technical matter, it needed careful understanding:

> This situation has its distressing as well as comical aspects, as well as its serious ones. It is also determined by so many and such complicated factors, it is so unavoidable and so difficult to clear up, that a discussion of it to meet a vital need of analytic technique has long been overdue (p. 159).

During the period when he wrote those words, Freud was still concerned with his colleague, Breuer's, difficulties in dealing with the transference love of Anna O., a passion so inflamed as to have unnerved even the rather staid

Mrs. Breuer. Eventually, Breuer felt he had to flee the passionate outpourings of Anna O. Freud, in his consideration of that case, ruminates that the nature of such love is so exceptional that, should it occur between doctor and patient, it may lead to marriage (infrequently, though Otto Fenichel married his patient) or, more reasonably, to the need to transfer the patient in question. Thus, Freud considered transference love as parallel to love outside the treatment situation and as a most impelling force to contend with within the treatment as well.

He also hints of the possibility of gratifying transference love during the treatment by allowing the possibility of entering into an illicit union with the patient for a short duration; but he sees professional and conventional morality in opposition to such an option and notes any such allowance as, in any case, at odds with his treatment based, as it is, upon interpretation as opposed to the acting out, of the archaic roots of neurosis. Indeed, in another classic paper on technique, Freud (1912) had argued that both the negative and erotic transferences were resistances to treatment and that only the sublimated positive transference was the proper vehicle to move the treatment along by allowing the patient to be able to withstand the shocks of interpretation. In his later papers on technique, Freud rests assured that transference love, occasioned by the unique characteristics of the analytic situation, is a phenomenon occurring without fail in such circumstances and is the cornerstone of psychoanalytic cure.

That he attributed such value to his emerging concept of transference love and its place in psychoanalysis is further substantiated by his warning to analysts against preparing the patient for its emergence within the treatment saying, to do so, robs the patient of the necessary affective spontaneity crucial for the therapeutic effect of transference interpretations: "... I can hardly imagine a more senseless proceeding" (p. 161). The beginnings of such feelings towards the doctor are usually heralded by the patient's feeling he or she is falling in love with the doctor; but with the reduction of symptoms so too, he notes, goes the transference love. The power of such love cannot be underestimated, however, and Freud notes that it may be responsible for an elevation of mood and feeling of well-being that heralds a temporary "transference cure", a situation the analyst needs to be on guard for. He also cautions the unsuspecting analyst to be on guard for the more passionate patient's utilizing her transference love to attempt to control the authority of the doctor and thus further the course of resistance. Of this he says:

> ... the resistance is acting as an *agent provocateur*; it heightens the patient's
> state of being in love and exaggerates her readiness for sexual surrender in or-
> der to justify the working of repression all the more emphatically, by pointing to
> the dangers of such licentiousness (p. 163).

Freud, seemingly somewhat conflicted at times in his discussion of transference love, nonetheless, wishes to stand on the side of the analyst's repression of his own responses to it rather than giving into gratification of them.
He says the analyst may not accept or return tender feelings. When the patient
acts upon them too uninhibitedly, he says she needs to be reminded of "social
morality"! Does it not seem somewhat contradictory, however, that Freud in
instructing us that transference love is the cornerstone of psychoanalysis (the
way to overcoming neurotic resistance), is also concerned to combat it by in-
voking social morality? How would such advice to weigh in on the side of social convention affect the way analysts conduct treatment today?

Of course, Freud was inclined to take a middle path allowing that tender feelings could be expressed but not acted upon by any more physical forms of expression. But even this more limited venue of gratification might be seen, especially in the context in which he way theorizing and practicing, as too seductive:
first, it opened a door to greater possible transgression and, secondly, given the
methodological assumptions of Cartesian subjectivity, allowed an unnecessary
intrusion upon the effectiveness of the method of psychoanalytic technique. The
latter followed from Freud's view that each psyche is fundamentally a closed (in
the sense of being an intra-psychic) system, from which he concluded it would
be, from the standpoint of psychoanalytic technique, unnecessarily intrusive for
the analyst to take any but a completely neutral and abstemious relation to the
patient; remaining a blank screen, as it were, upon which to allow the patient to
project (transfer) the objects of his or her internal life. The idea of subjectivity
being a fundamentally closed, intra-psychic system, the psychological version of
the doctrine of Cartesian subjectivity, is, however, a view hotly contested in today's climate of more intersubjectivist concepts of subjectivity. But in Freud's
time, and for Freud as well, it was a very compelling and rather uncritically accepted methodological assumption about the nature of human subjectivity and,
in his case, underlay the whole edifice of psychoanalysis itself. Thus, Freud was
able to liken himself (and psychoanalysts in general) to being surgeons per-
forming an operation where relational matters of personality were not only irrelevant but were also inappropriate to the successful conduct of a psychoanalytic treatment that depended upon the neutrality of "curing" interpretations by
the analyst. The futility of responding to the needs of the patient over and above
his need to be cured was expressed by Freud in an anecdote cited by him to the
effect that: there once was a free-thinking insurance agent whom, on his
deathbed, his family wished him to see a pastor. The latter came and spent so
much time with the sick man that hopes arose that he might return to life. Alas,
when the pastor came out of the sick room, the pastor had been insured by the
insurance agent, but the insurance agent had not been converted by the pastor
and had died.

Freud's final recipe for dealing with transference love in the analytic situation will sound unreal as there is no corresponding model for it in real life. His recommendation is that the analyst not steer away from it, nor be repulsed by it, nor in any way make it seem distasteful; but, rather, must "resolutely withhold any response to it". His reasoning, logical and clear, was based upon the assumption that such love was a symptom that needed to be analyzed and the patient needed to be encouraged to tell all he could bring to mind about it:

> . . . all her preconditions for loving, all her fantasies springing from her sexual desires, all the detailed characteristics of her state of being in love, to come to light; and from these she will let herself open the way to the infantile roots of her love (p. 166).

It is to be noted that Freud vacillates between stating that love in the therapeutic situation of analysis is no different in kind from love in real life and the contrary proposition that there exists no model in real life for the love that manifests itself in the unique circumstances of the analytic situation. He is also unclear about the seemingly contradictory advice to analysts recommending a free flowing spontaneity on the part of their patients while, when necessary, admixing it with a tincture of moral repression. The either/or nature of this observation, in line with Freud's rather linear, topographic understanding, may, however, be part of the problem here as it does not, as he does not, consider the "scientific" legitimacy of exploring what happens "in between in the analytic encounter".

An exception to this, however, is suggested by the example Freud brings up, but does not fully address in these terms, of certain female patients of extraordinary passion. ". . . These are women of elemental passionate-ness who tolerate no surrogates" (p.166). They demand their love to be returned or else display the full enmity of a woman scorned. Freud does not tackle this problem in the way that we, in observing as part of the problem with some of his conclusions on this matter the rather either/or construction of the technical issues involved; but, finds, rather, another occasion to muse upon the way such persons develop a capacity for neurosis joined with an intractable need for love. He describes such patients as processed of violent temperaments which he sees as resistance to adopting an analytic attitude following from the fact that ". . . [she] is used to such men as so excite her (including original love objects) [and who] demand that from her" (p. 166). On the other hand, we are informed that "real love", love outside, but embodied within the analytic attitude as well, is more appropriately manifest in women by more docile, submissive tendencies in the transference towards men (giving up resistance, as it were, to a more taking attitude of the man and what he has to give her). For

Freud, again in this rather more either/or vein, such temperamental women who take a different position in the transference are seen, by their rebellious spirit, to have no interest in their treatment nor have any respect for their doctor's well founded opinion. How does this attitude help, though, in the need to help such women in moderating and transforming their "rebellious love" into a more modulated expression? Freud can't or, at any rate, doesn't answer this; but he does move on to consider the question once and for all, as it were, whether and to what extent love within the analytic situation is not also "real love'.

The argument takes the tack that, in the end, transference love really is a species of "real love". This is how the argument goes. Although transference love is a form of resistance, it is really only a form of aim-inhibited love; that is, its infantile roots have been sublimated or aim-inhibited to allow expression in terms of affectionate feelings for the analyst (the basis for what would later be known as the analytic working alliance). Thus, its roots are no more lacking in the need for repetition of infantile love objects than is manifest in any form of love. Indeed, asking how the genuineness of love can be recognized Freud replies by saying: look at its efficacy, its serviceability, its capacity in achieving its love aim. In this, he says, ". . . transference love seems to be second to none; one has the impression that one could obtain anything from it" (p. 168). He concludes, then, by saying that the state of being in love while in analytic treatment has all the hallmarks of real love and differs only in that it occurs in analysis, is intensified by resistance and is lacking in regard for reality.

During this whole discussion, the reader may be made to feel slightly uncomfortable by Freud's discomfort through the entirety of his rather extended treatment of the topic of transference love. Clearly, the concept created tensions for him as it threatened the very staid moral climate of early twentieth century Vienna. How, indeed, in such a climate, was one to sell the idea of a cure that relied upon "falling in love with one's doctor" as a necessary enactment to work through aspects of infantile incestuous sexual wishes for ones parents, siblings and guardians? Not an easy case to make during that time or, for that matter, in any time, to be sure. So Freud heavily relied upon making analogies to medical practice and ethics. (He was also, of course, an M.D.) His message is, and rightly, that although analysts may be sorely tempted to succumb to responding to such love, the warning is that to do so violates the treatment by violating the doctor/patient relationship: ". . . [f]or the doctor, ethical motives unite with the technical ones to restrain him from giving the patient his love" (p.169). Yet Freud is hyperaware of the impelling force of love:

Those who are still youngish and not yet bound by strong ties may in particular find it a hard task. Sexual love is undoubtedly one of the chief things in life, and the union of mental and bodily satisfaction in the enjoyment of love is one of its culminating peaks (p. 169).

Again, though Freud speaks here of the transference and countertransference, he is not under-estimating the impelling quality of the emotional experience of transference love both for doctor and patient, but is warning of the pitfalls to the treatment if the doctor surrenders to it. Central to his position is that, in so much as transference love is a species of "real love", it is easy for the doctor to feel the seduction to respond. Yet, clearly, to do so in the uneven power relationship of the analytic situation, would be a violation of the subject-ness of the patient and, hence, of her subjectivity. Moreover, it would be in complete violation of the treatment. Thus the difference of the real-love aspect of the transference love within the analytic situation and of real love outside of an analytic situation, is just that: transference love occurs within a context of treatment and is invoked for the purpose of treatment while transferential love, as it were, outside of an analytic situation is just "real love"; that is, love occurring outside of a context of treatment. If one does not confuse these two realms, there can be no question of what is and what is not permitted from within the relationship between doctor and patient defined by the analytic situation.

An interesting side line to this discussion about the nature and permissible limits of transference love relatedness, perhaps, is the fact that it occurs within a broader discussion not only of the healing power of love within the analytic situation, but also of the healing power of love in general. Also, however, it speaks to the neurotic and even psychotic consequences of the failure of love. Just for starters, do we not find at the root of all depressions, for example, disappointed love? And are not many anxiety symptoms due to the fear of losing love? The list goes on. So when Freud called analysis a reeducation, a process we note as facilitated by the love in transference loving, are we not closer to the truth if we redefine it as an education in the art of learning how to love again?

Now, the idea that love is involved in cure is not new in psychoanalysis. Often, though, it is not talked about with any degree of prominence or is hidden by various other theoretical concerns. Even those following more relational or intersubjectivist schools of psychoanalytic thought, though love may make an appearance in their discussion (witness, for example the work of Gilligan and Benjamin discussed above), nonetheless, it is often not brought out in the full sense of "falling in love" in the manner discussed by Freud as we have seen. Others, however, have made it more of a lynch-pin to their overall psychoanalytic position.

PSYCHOANALYSIS AND THE CURATIVE POWER OF "EROS"

Any exploration of the effects of Eros in psychoanalysis needs to commence with consideration of the contributions to the subject by Georg Groddeck, followed closely by considering those of Sandor Ferenzci, an analyst whose technical innovations to the practice of psychoanalysis in the early years of its development have been enjoying somewhat of a renaissance lately. To begin, Georg Groddeck was a physician and son of a physician who lived from 1866 to 1934. He showed disdain for medical orthodoxy and was an admirer of Freud and psychoanalysis. However, he was a different kind of analyst employing a method different from Freud's that relied upon free association. He made use of deep massage and dieting in his sanatorium in Baden-Baden, but he eschewed cursory acquaintance with his patients in a context merely of prescribing medications, preferring, instead, to take a deep personal interest in each of his patients. He had astonishing success with patients suffering from chronic symptoms, abandoned by others as incurable.

He viewed psychopathology as having more to do with a person's life-style rather than from the effects of organic dysfunction and viewed the doctor-patient relationship as the most important factor in the treatment. He came to realize the overarching influence of unconscious symbolism in the formation of symptoms and attempted to explain its dynamics in his book, *The Book of the It* (1961). In this work he explains how it is that all thought and action are the unavoidable consequence of unconscious symbolization while the 'It' is the force binding and linking symbols together. In all other respects his treatment resembled more orthodox aspects of traditional psychoanalytic psychotherapy. Yet the synthesis of relational, and meta-psychological divergences associated with his theory of the 'It' produced a quite original psychoanalytic hybrid.

In his own words, Groddeck explained the 'It' as conscious and unconscious combined, holding sway over both brain and consciousness itself. In his view there is no opposition between an 'Ego' and the 'It', as the 'Ego' is a phenomenon of the 'It', the life force that figures in the determination of all of our actions. It starts at the moment of fertilization and dies with the individual's last breath. Ambiguous as to gender, containing both male and female elements, it is in perpetual motion and asserts itself in moods it seeks to rationalize by seeking confirmation in the 'outer world' from 'reality-based' perception. It has needs and capacities for love and hate.

In Groddeck's view, Man creates his own illness and suffering for the sake of pleasure; for suffering is the guilt-assuaging (and, therefore relieving) reaction to guilt and its associated need for punishment; and in that relief from guilt our suffering gives us a sort of gratification, pleasure. In this sense, Groddeck sees illness as yet another symbolic manifestation of the 'It', the underlying and all-over source of pleasure. In this regard, Groddeck posits two events as primary in shaping life prefigured as it is out of the 'It'. The first such shaping factor arises out of the masturbatory sensations experienced from early childhood while the second arises out of the ever-lasting yearning to return to the protective surround of the maternal experienced in infancy. Illness, in its tendency for relief by seeking return to the symbiotic warmth of the maternal, is both auto-erotic and regressive. Thus, it satisfies both of these two fundamental shaping parameters of the 'It' expressed in the pleasure state of auto-erotic return. For the purposes of cure (if, indeed, such as this has a cure), all depends less upon technical interpretation than upon accurately deciphering the messages from the 'It'. Indeed, Groddeck believed that decoding the symbolic manifestations of the 'It' must prefigure any interpretation and is essential in treating all sickness whether mental or physical. Thus, he proposed, there must be a psychoanalytic dimension to all treatment of illness.

Groddeck's therapeutic technique consisted of creating a maternal environment in the analytic situation by attempting to duplicate the early mother's interest and care. For example, he cured an agoraphobic man not just by being available as his doctor but, also, by joining him on walks. As he saw no antagonism between 'Ego' and 'It', 'reality' and 'fantasy' blended and folded into each other creating a pulsating rhythmic texture to life. He expressed it as an endless capacity for receiving, transforming and giving forth: impregnation, conception and labor; the buzzing, pulse of life reproduced, as well, in consciousness itself.

He thought that some analysts placed too much emphasis upon direct sexual satisfaction and saw the latter as just another, but not necessarily privileged, manifestation of the many and diverse rhythms of life arising out of the 'It'. However, he was not unaware of the force of the erotic drive and noted that its explosive power could be a force in the creation of new beauty or, on the contrary, could ravage and destroy. Yet, he did not reduce the erotic to mere genital excitement, but saw it always a more powerful domain out of which activity arises the symbols of all life: love, birth and death.

He thought, however, that love had little to do with erotic passion and was a much broader concept. Thus, feelings of love could be evinced by many experiences other than just that of being in the presence of one's beloved. He noted that even lovers are only occasionally passionate. Love, for Groddeck, was more the sense of tranquil equilibrium which, when it disappears in the ferment of passion, gives way to forces that are so incomprehensible that we can only think them as magic. Moreover, there is no 'first love' or 'first desire'. The past always stands next to the future and a symbol in its manifold significance can never be known. But to live fully we must own the symbol because the symbol is Life itself:

> In very truth, the myth is truth, symbolic truth, while reality is error. The man who learns to see the symbol will laugh at the talk about a Reality Principle, even if he honors and loves Freud, as I do (p. 268).

Now Freud knew Groddeck and was aware of his opinions. He, too, believed that Eros was a necessary ingredient of the analytic endeavor. However, very much aware of Breuer's famous case of Anna O., he was well aware of how such strong feelings could wreak havoc in analysis. He, therefore, sought to confine such feelings to within the controlled arena of the transference alone and cautioned analysts to assume neutrality within the analytic situation, so that the appearance of such erotic awakenings could be analyzed away more as artificial expressions of the transference rather than real in terms of their object. But Groddeck's recommendation that the analyst take a more active role in the analytic situation remained alive in the work of Ferenczi.

In turning our attention upon Ferenczi, it is perhaps most helpful to begin with Martin Bergmann's (1976) description of the man:

> He was brilliant, intuitive and empathetic as well as being a keen observer. He reported that he soon developed a reputation for working with hopeless cases. He had a remarkable ability to speak in or reproduce the language of children. Socially, he was warm, charming, gregarious, witty, and perhaps impulsive. He was quick tempered, but also quick to forgive (p. 46).

Freud was quite taken by Ferenczi and invited him to go on vacation with him as well as to accompany him to the famous Clarke University conclave. In addition, Ferenczi undertook an analysis with Freud.

Though some of his papers were praised by Freud as being of "pure analytic gold", Ferenczi soon began to grapple with the possibility of taking a more active stance in the analytic situation, a position that began to distance him from a more Freudian orthodoxy. For example, like Rank, he advocated utilizing the transference more to facilitate abreaction than merely to solicit recollection of childhood memories. For cases considered incurable, cases with significant early trauma, he even advocated modifying the analytic environment in ways that, by promoting corrective emotional experiences, aimed to repair original trauma so as to prepare the patient for later more traditional analytic techniques. Thus, he sometimes sat patients on his lap, kissed them or gently stroked them in a therapeutic effort to re-start psychic growth. Moreover, Ferenczi believed that Freud's more abstemious analytic approach was especially unsuited to promote character change.

Interestingly, Freud (1919) was not unaware of these limits to his technique and acknowledged that treatment of obsessional neuroses as well as phobias required a more active analytic stance than the more abstemious or deprivational approach designed for the treatment of hysteria, the original condition for which the more conservative psychoanalytic approach of classical psychoanalysis had been invented to cure. Thus, even Freud concluded that the pure gold of analysis would have to be alloyed at times with the copper of direct suggestion; nor would he rule out hypnosis in cases of 'war neuroses'.

Returning to Ferenczi, though, it is possible that he knew of Groddeck's work and was influenced by it. We do know, for example, when he became sick at the end of his life, that he sought treatment at Groddeck's sanitarium. To begin with, however, Ferenczi was a diligent student of Freud's and adhered to the technique of neutrality in the analysis of a patient's free associations. In a paper of 1919 entitled *"Technical Difficulties in the Analysis of a Case of Hysteria"*, reporting on a treatment that became mired in an erotic transference, Ferenczi noted that by stopping and then re-starting the analysis while encouraging her to speak about her fantasy life but prohibiting any masturbatory activity, he was able to induce an infantile neurosis that could then be analyzed, the results of which ended in less sexual inhibition with her husband. In his following paper of 1921, Ferenczi insisted that he had not altered analytic technique in his treatment of such patients, but had simply introduced parameters that helped the patient to comply with the technique. In short, he encouraged such patients to exaggerate their neurotic condition by soliciting infantile fantasy while opposing its masturbatory enactment; a process that resulted in other memories coming to the surface that then, via analysis and abreaction, resulted in a diminution of the hysterical symptoms.

He then moved on to trying this technique in the realm of the more aggressive fantasies associated with the Oedipal situation. Here, again, the idea was to solicit these fantasies so that the patient could more nearly re-experience the trauma in an abreactional analytic frame. In 1930, however, in a paper entitled *"The Principle of Relaxation and Neocatharsis"*, he broke more openly with Freud by emphasizing the need for patients to experience a genuinely cathartic experience at the end of analysis if the advances made in their analyses were to be fully consolidated in a structure with permanent stability.

He also believed that traumatic sexual experiences in childhood created conditions for primal repression that could produce psychotic-like states of mind replete with hallucinatory memory contents. Moreover, he believed these memories could only be brought out in analysis through the production of a facilitating environment where analyst and analysand were caught up in replicating a corrective infantile environment in contrast to the original more toxic infantile environment. Only then could such memories become integrated in a more mature (less regressive) psychic structuring. In his famous paper of 1933 on the confusion of tongues between patient and analyst, he even suggested the idea that with such patients, analyst and analysand needed to be caught up in what amounted to a mutual analysis together in forging such reconstructive facilitating environments. Unfortunately, perhaps, as this procedure did not put limits upon potential self-disclosure by the analyst, Ferenczi was excluded from the psychoanalytic establishment.

His impact, however, has been profound and far-reaching. Balint (1968) in his book, *The Basic Fault*, for example, agrees with Ferenczi that in order to heal the trauma at the point where the environment failed the patient, the analyst must facilitate regression in the patient back to this fault line, as it were, before further analytic work is possible. Balint also believes that it was Ferenczi who first established the two-person (non-Cartesian) psychology that laid the groundwork for modern object relations psychoanalytic theory. Moreover, both Kohut and Spotnitz borrowed from Ferenczi in their later detailing of narcissistic pathology, especially from the standpoint of technique where both found helpful hints from the ways Ferenczi first trail-blazed in his efforts to defeat stagnation in the analytic situation. Moreover, Ferenczi's emphasis upon activity in the analytic relationship, laid the groundwork for modern behavioral and gestalt techniques while his idea of the need to create a nurturing environment in the analytic situation anticipated Winnicott's famous notion of the "facilitating environment".

There have been other psychoanalysts with ideas similar to those which, sparked by Ferenczi, influenced the development of British object relations psychoanalysis and have reconfigured the way in which 'love' is viewed from within psychoanalytic treatment. Others less sympathetic to this development have, nonetheless, relied upon it in interesting ways in developing their own ideas about the place of 'love' in psychoanalysis. Thus, for example, the theories of R.D. Laing, a Scottish psychiatrist and psychoanalyst, (given prominent place over the years in the *Psychoanalytic Review),* whose views, not unlike those of the British object relations school he often felt unsympathetic to, regarded love as a life or death ingredient in treating cases of acute mental or physical illness. He observed that even in the most disturbed of patients, love never ceases to exist and becomes even more important when requests for it are so distorted and contorted by the "rubble" of psychotic language that it is hardly knowable any longer.

According to Thompson (2000), Laing's ideas about love and its importance were based in part upon Biblical references. Thus, he believed that the failure to realize our most fundamental potential as human beings was due to our indifference, often, in following the maxim *love thy neighbor as thyself*, an indifference resulting in a disowning of our human destiny. For Laing, health and happiness is intrinsically connected to recognition of the sanctity of the otherness of the other person. Consequently, pathology can never be thought of as separate from a context of relatedness and, so, must always be conceptualized as a certain *dysfunction in relationship*. Because, according to Gans (2000), Laing believed that to live up to human potential means to overcome the contingencies and constraints in realizing loving relatedness, he never thought that severe pathology could be caused by fear of death; but, rather, felt it was rooted in fear of loss of primordial love. He felt the anticipation of such loss was an experience that lay the groundwork, as it were, to an underlying vulnerability afflicting innumerable persons and was especially reinforced in those who, insecure in love from within the early family system, learned to feel others as threatening or engulfing. Such persons begin from a very early age to experience themselves as outcasts unable to comply with family and social norms.

Laing noted that families are often violent systems enforcing compliance to family norms and roles through coercion, pretending such violence to be about love. This has a terribly corrosive effect upon the capacity of such victims to be in touch with innocent, tender feelings, so crucial if love is to resonate in sexual love with the more subtle sources and expression of its exquisite pleasure. Because family members internalize reciprocally their roles within the system, these internalizations come to govern the interpersonal defense systems that come to regulate and reinforce pathological relatedness and, later, congeal into what some have called character defenses deep within identity. Paradoxically, then, any sense of separating from such pathological systems becomes a source of acute annihilation anxiety in terms of fear in losing core identity. Indeed, in my practice, I have observed the terror of such depressed and anxious persons when they can no longer identify with their pathological family roots and experience growth in agency and themselves as a loss of identity. We might explain this as an acute sense of fear of loss of self-love (core identity) caused by the concomitant loss of super-ego love, the internalized scene of family pathology. Laing rightly sees it as consequent to corruption of love by power relations starting with the family that, continuing in the institutions of state and society, all work against the realization of the more tender nature of love and loving.

If pathology is born of distortions in the ability of a person to express and realize himself through love and loving, while the capacity for love and

loving is realizable only in relationship to another, it follows that psychotherapy, a pathway to the re-finding of one's relatedness in love, must be understood as an attempt by two people to recover such wholeness of being human
(love) through a relationship between them:

> Psychotherapy is the process of awakening from the hypnotic induction and
> trans-states of convention, the spell of the familiar, in order to reclaim responsi-
> bility for the way we see, and do not see, love and are unloving to our neighbors
> and ourselves (p. 542).

Although, as we have seen, Laing locates pathology in distortions in the individual's capacity to realize his love as a consequence of its distortion
through interactions with another (and hence beginning in the family system);
any possible deeper origins, if any need be identified, are less clear. He
speaks, though, of a primordial differentiation process beginning with the
voyage through the Fallopian tubes and ending in our placental surrounds. Is
it not possible that such primitive ordeals of survival during gestation leave
non-verbal imprints? And if it were so, would it not be possible that patterns
of prenatal experience are replayed in postnatal life?

While the idea of prenatal influences cannot be disregarded and have been
accepted by more physically oriented "scientific" understandings of our origins (for example, that we are fundamentally bisexual and only develop male
and female genital characteristics with the admixture of the 'y' chromosome),
nonetheless, his theories are not so much concerned with bio-physical etiol-
ogy as they are with the intersubjective roots of subjective experience especially as that relates to the issue of the interpersonal field and how that affects
the capacity for the realization, in each, of the need to love.

These ideas will seem very familiar, indeed, for those acquainted with the
work of many of today's leading relational psychoanalytic theorists who fore-
ground an emphasis upon the view of the intersubjective nature of mind and,
therefore, see much of the origins of pathology as consequent to systems of
dysfunctional relatedness. Kohut (1984) is seen by some as having started the
move in this country towards this intersubjectivist trend in American psychoanalysis; but its most vigorous early expression is to be found in the work of
Sullivan and the interpersonal psychoanalytic school he founded. Many others, including Mitchell and Aron (1999) have followed suit with their own
distinctive blends of interpersonal, object relational and intersubjectivist psychoanalytic philosophies all stemming from the insight that the psyche is inherently, from the get-go, a two-person system originating out of a two-person system or matrix, hence, not, as according to Freud, arising from a
one-person world of primary narcissism. Depending upon the particular the-

orist, other revisions to the psychoanalytic canon originated by Freud include shifting away from the dual instinct drive model of mind, the idea of the polarity between conscious and unconscious mind and, for some, even reliance upon the idea of repression and sublimation as the primary mechanisms underlying, respectively, pathology and health.

The shift from looking at pathology in terms of intrapsychic conflict alone to one where it is seen also from the standpoint of an interpersonal dimension of intersubjective relatedness, has had profound effects upon the way the psychoanalytic situation is viewed and theorized by such theorists. As the analyst is no longer seen as standing outside of the patient's pathology reflecting back, as it were, as from a blank screen aspects of the patient's conflict, the therapist is no longer able to discount the impact of his personality—itself a relational system—to the dynamics of the treatment. Thus, he is not the "know-all" doctor who interprets each act of the patient's resistance to the treatment (him!) as deriving from an infantile neurosis; but rather sees treatment as the unfolding of aspects of an inter-personal relationship; one that through, what Ogden (1994) has called the creation of a "third reality", is, as it were, a co-creation where both persons have contributed to, and changed the reality of, the other in the process of an unfolding dialogue, a dialogue where the ravages of hate are transformed by the modulations of love.

All of these revisions reflect the fact that psychoanalysis was an invention occurring within a certain time and place; that is, within a specific cultural-historical setting. Because of this fact, which is as much a fact of our times as of Freud's, the pronouncements of any age are not without biases specific to that setting. It must be remembered that in Freud's time, strict "Victorian" moral standards were causing unhappiness that, in some cases, were manifesting themselves in the bizarre behaviors of what was later understood as conversion symptoms of hysteria. Sexual repression, in adaptation to the demands of infantile neurosis, itself the cause of overly strict upbringing, was at the root not only of hysterical symptoms but of depression, anxiety and obsessive-compulsive acting out to name but a few of now commonly recognized such syndromes of psychic pain.

Freud's teachings signaled a revolution, a theory of liberation from these constraints, and a new respect for the rights of individual choice and personal freedom in determining and adopting one's own path to happiness and self-realization. At the same time, his teachings also occurred within a context of an educated Vienna, influenced by philosophy, religion and the arts. In such a conservative setting, Freud needed to protect his extraordinarily subversive ideas from the charge of heresy. As he was a scientist and a doctor (an M.D.), he did so by legitimating them within the scientific framework of the practice of medicine in his day. It was the assumptions of that framework, the assumptions of Cartesian mechanics, that colored his theorizations of subjectivity and the mechanics of mental functioning in ways that left him open, in a later time, to charges of creating a solipsistic, mechanistic view of the workings of mental life in contra-distinction to a more intersubjectivist understanding of mind from within a non-Cartesian standpoint. In particular, it is his idea of psychic development originating in the solipsistic point of departure of primary narcissism that has created the impression that his view of the mind was fundamentally Cartesian.

Today's non-Cartesian alternative, in opposition to Descartes' famous dictum that self-conscious awareness cannot rationally include certainty of other minds (and so can not include any such as intrinsic to one's own self-conscious awareness), asserts just the opposite: namely, that subjectivity conceived as intrinsically unrelated to another's subjectivity (the doctrine of primary narcissism or solipsistic subjectivity) is incoherent. That is, relationalists of all stripes reject the view of solipsistic subjectivity (the implicit implication of the doctrine of primary narcissism) thought to follow from Descartes' famous maxim, *cogito ergo sum*: that one's self experience alone, the 'I' of the cogito, is the only certainty of anything existing other than the 'I' given in the experience of 'I'; therefore, since that experience does not include within it anything other than the 'I' intrinsic to such self-conscious awareness alone, it must be possible, then, to doubt the existence of every thing outside of the experience of that self-experience (the 'I' of self-conscious awareness alone), whose existence is asserted—and therefore proven—even in the act of trying to doubt it.

Today's relationalists, then, reject not only the doctrine of primary narcissism and the solipsistic subjectivity it entails, but also the way Freud fused this idea with his mechanistic-corpuscular theory of mental functioning that viewed the mind as akin to a sort of hydraulic mechanical system responding to and transferring pressures (drive derivatives) according to adaptations furthered by internal compromise formations among competing pressures (impulses from structures in conflict) in order to allow, as it were, hydro-static states of equilibrium within an organization (an intra-psychic system) viewed essentially in isolation from other such systems (persons), but with whom there is a need to interact in order, primarily, to discharge energy so as to achieve a return to equilibrium (gratification) through such discharge (interaction). Many such relationalists who now turn away from these more "scientistic" leanings of Freud's Cartesian-mechanistic view of mind, first came upon an alternative point of departure from the more intersubjective vocabulary of 'being' created by phenomenological philosophers in Europe, such as Husserl and Heiddeger (his pupil), who were writing during the same period that Freud's was creating his "science" of psychoanalysis.

According to Thompson (2000), Laing too, believing a heartless, mechanistic science of mind could only lead to soul destroying practice, turned to the different point of departure offered by phenomenological philosophy in an effort to find a better pathway to building an understanding of the mysteries of mind in terms of a more intersubjective model, one that situated subjectivity in a web of human relatedness. In this search for new meanings to build a more humane psychology, he rejected the life of routine convention as a sort of loveless slumber, finding ordinary life more akin to trance-like illusion than a profound experience of 'being'. In his retreat from such an ordinary frame of reference, he appropriated aspects of Husserl's philosophical approach that insisted the only reality we know we know through its experience in consciousness. Likewise, Laing asks us to attend to our own acts of consciousness in order to explore the meaning of our experience.

In directing us in this way, Laing is not suggesting a flight from "the objective", since all that is objective is also first an experience of consciousness; rather by embracing aspects of a phenomenological method, he is pointing out that every 'thing', both 'subjective' and 'objective', is first presented to us as a content of consciousness; and we can explore that act of consciousness as a realm of reality that pre-figures the question of the 'thing' separate from consciousness. In psychology, too, we need less to be taken up with questions of structures of mind in relation to hidden forces of repression and such and more concerned to better understand the meaning that our subjectivity has for us in grounding our sense of 'being'. One such meaning we discover in this way, according to Laing, is that the sense of a mind/body dichotomy is really a misleading construction of intellectualization; for our body, according to Laing, is the heart and source of our mind—which is the body, as it were, speaking itself as consciousness.

Laing was also influenced by other philosophical orientations. For example, he was very impressed by Martin Buber's (1970) *I and Thou*. When working on a neurological unit, for instance, he became convinced that the nervous systems of different patients were influenced by each other. Indeed, not unlike Buber's insight in his famous elucidation of the *I and Thou*, there seemed an application in terms of the interplay between two physiologies as well. Added to the influence of Buber and Husserl mentioned above, there was also the influence of Heidegger, Husserl's pupil, and the place of "Dasein-analytics" in a developing existentialist approach to understanding the psychology of mind.

Indeed, existential analysis of the sort developed in part in the work of Laing was primarily based upon the writings of the German philosopher, Martin Heidegger. (In America, Rollo May (2004) became one of the most prominent existentialist analysts based in this tradition.) Ludwig Binswanger (2004) of whom we spoke earlier, described existential analysis as exploring a person's world map from the phenomenological (or intentional standpoint) of experience by which the person interacts with the world. The focus of such an exploration is on the interaction of environment and self to form a "life-world", the frame of intersubjective relatedness. Meaning is derived from realizing how we are 'in-the-world' and how we need to transcend our being-in-the-world as a mere factic (or ontic, as Heidegger put it) reality in order to engage more deeply our "ontological" nature.

Transcendence in German means "a going over and across" and, hence, of bridging difference. Thus, when properly focused upon our ontological nature in transcendence of mere facticity, we are able to bridge dichotomies such as subject/object and self/world in order to more deeply appreciate Being, the source (a sort of enigmatic underlying Erotic force) of existence.

Heidegger was especially influenced by the pre-Socratic philosopher, Heraclitus, who said that in a state of wakening, we all have a world in common whereas, in contrast, when we dream, we turn to a world of our own. The idea of transcendence allows a way of coping with the shared world we all inhabit while allowing a more individualized, or subjective, immersion in that world through the specific modes of being that define the subjective world of self-in-interaction. This sense of subjectivity, as true of everything else experienced from within an emotional spectrum, has dual aspects. Thus, for example, it can be either experienced as unconscious dependency or individual freedom. But the relation of one's world-view and its interaction with modes of self is never static: it is always in a process of being reacquired and reaffirmed in a process of self-generation.

As in modern-day systems theory, everything is connected with everything else in an organic unity such that no change in one part of the system leaves unaffected any other part of the whole. Such a view of the subject of inquiry, from a psychological standpoint, means that the methods of the natural sciences and the ontological assumptions it makes in application to the objects it studies are completely out of sync with subjects understood in this "existential" terms. Thus, the whole importance, from within the methodological framework of such natural science, of facts and the accumulation of facts by which to arrive at inductive conclusions, gives way, instead, to a process of ". . . lovingly delving into the nature and context of the single phenomenon" (p. 200).

Existential analysis, in many ways a systematic alternative self-understanding to the more mechanistic "scientistic" framework of Freudian psychoanalysis, includes a concept of "existential anxiety" that, developed in part by Heidegger and amplified upon by Sartre (the famous French existentialist writer of the last century), recognizes, as part of the natural limit of mortality, a sense of naked horror at the prospect of the end of subjectivity in death. In this connection, Laing, as well, points out, in agreement with Heidegger, that not all hurts and disappointments are caused by others, but are influenced, as well, by the limits of our existence and the impact of a geophysical world. Thus, "death anxiety" which has often been referred to as the basis for this "existential anxiety" situates all finite beings within a context of 'limit' and, so, creates the common destiny (or horizon) to the 'being-in-the-world' for beings such as we.

David Mann (1966), an English psychoanalyst, wrote on the influence of subjectivity in the analytic relationship, but from a less existentialist point of departure. The title of his book, *Psychotherapy—an Erotic Relationship*, bluntly puts the topic of transference love and countertransference love back on the table for re-examination. He says both concepts are about:

> . . . how the erotic has significance in the analytic relationship between patient and therapist. To summarize [my] whole book in a single sentence: I consider that the erotic pervades most if not all psychoanalytic encounters and is largely a positive and transformational influence (p. 1).

He accounts for his thesis by making reference to data from infant observation that informs us about both the mind of the infant and of the relevance of mythology. Myths, he tells us, are tales informing us of Man's deepest preoccupations throughout recorded history. They enrich clinical data by informing us of meanings shaping development that are implicit, deep within the fabric of *human experience.*

With regard to the role of 'the erotic' in understanding psychoanalytic practice, he is highly critical of analytic tenets that regard 'the erotic' as mere resistance created by the psychoanalytic situation—as though, therefore, it was not also something genuine.

One cannot help but explore the erotic from observing two lovers, each seeking a transformation via erotic and love experiences. Mann employs this model to the analytic encounter. An erotic transference would symbolize that the patient is trying to change at the deepest self level. The erotic then is located and described as emerging from an interactional matrix.

Not unlike other analysts we have looked at in this regard, Mann believes that the source of erotic life is to be found in the relationship between infant and mother. As experiences widen during development, it remains the most treasured experience, but one that leads both to 'wonder' and tragedy. Though painful, it is psychically binding.

Returning again to the theme of mythology in understanding psychic life, Mann notes that in Greek mythology, Eros was the first of the gods: ". . . without him, none of the rest could have been born". He is equated with the life-stimulating sun and the created life on earth; and, as such, he is seen as a life-affirming and creative force, of love, rather than a god of sexual lust. He notes, however, it was only after another son was born to Aphrodite, Anteros—the god of passion, that Eros could grow up. It was then that he then fell in love with Psyche who became the personification of the "soul". Thus, the erotic is the creative force out of which is born both passion and soul. But if Eros, the name of 'love', is not connected with sexual passion, lust, then how is it that Eros comes to personify both the passion of creation (sexuality) and of 'love', the life-affirming glue that, as it were, binds the soul (psyche).

Mann considers the problem and offers the solution that both Eros and 'love' need to be understood rather more loosely than the way they have been configured in some psychoanalytic circles where they are seen as distinct and even at odds. He offers the solution that "out of the heat of passion (lust) old links are weakened so that new links can be forged (love)". Sexual passion, then, dissolves while 'love' binds and both are part of Eros. Thus, we need to understand that 'love' works its way through 'the erotic'. He proposes, however, that the concept of the erotic be primarily understood as a psychological rather than physical notion even though, as we have seen, it is usually, and rightly, associated with sexual excitement. Indeed, making reference to the anthropologist, Bataille (1957), Mann (1966) notes that while the erotic is a psychological experience, it is not independent of sexual aims that include reproduction and the desire for children:

> I am not, therefore, limiting the erotic to sexual arousal. The erotic may include fascination, disgust, or incestuous desire, which we may consider in Kumin's (1985) term as "erotic horror" (p. 6).

Yet in its primarily psychological sense, the erotic is the force that, moving development, tends towards a process of individualization, and, via differentiation, to greater autonomy in the realization of ever more advanced, comprehensive and complex states of differentiated unity (growth).

Returning to the significance of the maternal environment of the infant-mother dyad, Mann says the analytic encounter in the analytic situation is, in many respects, analogous to the relational environment of such an infant-mother dyad and that the psychological development between the two becomes, as it were, the 'analytic child'. The analogy is also pregnant with other meaning, however, as it also, and quite naturally, introduces aspects of a prohibited relationship fueled, as it is, by incestuous wishes. Thus, at the center of the analytic experience is a prohibited erotic desire that reproduces itself in the dynamics of the Oedipal scenario, which creates both the greatest of dangers while, simultaneously, allowing the possibility for the greatest release of creative potential; for it is the erotic that provides the fuel allowing the means of self- transformation that is the heart of analytic work and the soul of love.

Mann quotes the sociologist, McDougall, who notes that a developing child must also come to terms with the impossibility of the wish to incorporate both sexes and to possess both parents. He has to come to grips with the fact of mono-sexuality, as it were, and renounce his bisexual longings by finding other compensations. Interestingly, this position and the situation it depicts, brings to mind the aforementioned theme, discussed earlier, from Plato's *Symposium* where, it will be remembered, Aristophanes proposes that once people consisted of two-headed spheres incorporating both sexes who, split asunder by the jealous gods, forever thereafter engaged in an endless search to recover their lost unity. Thus, we see that erotic fantasy seeks to heal old wounds and to transform the individual by incorporating ever more complex and comprehensive degrees of unity in differentiation, a wish not just about recovering a past unity (in that case an undifferentiated one), but one that is directed towards the future in terms of building a new unity (a differentiated one). The backward related wish, born out of the compulsion endlessly to repeat, is regressive while the forward related wish, driven by the need for self-realization through growth and development, is progressive and is fueled by Eros.

The analytic situation and a patient's wish for growth announces a passionate juncture in the life of such an individual, where the compulsion to repeat the old is confronted by the desire for self- transformation and growth. The analytic situation provides a transitional space wherein this passionate dual between these two forces can be carried out. Here, the mother is a force in the background, as it were, while the "analytic child" is able to separate from, and integrate, her (and the Oedipal scene she conjures up) in ways that lead beyond it to greater degrees of self-realization through consolidation, integration and development (growth).

In all of this, the analyst acts as the focus for the patient's wish for self-transformation. He is the new transformational object, replacing the mother — but resonant with her, creating a conduit that allows, by facilitating conditions necessary for, intra-psychic change. Like a good-enough mother, all of this requires the analyst's empathy and love of the patient if the patient is to be reborn. Thus it depends upon the creative and transformational force of Eros. Yet if such transference love becomes a source of resistance, Mann warns that such an interruption in the treatment may be due more to the analyst's fear and anxiety lest passions become too great in the transference, rather than from the source of the resistance itself, transference love.

In this connection, Mann tries to sort out the source to the analyst's resistance to letting in such transference love as is occasioned by an erotic transference, by tracing it back to the case of Anna O. and Breuer's reaction to it. The latter, as you may recall, was frightened by Anna's fantasies, obviously felt guilty and responsible for them, and talked to his wife about them who became jealous and morose. Likewise, when Freud spoke to his wife, Martha, about it, she, too, became concerned lest Anna O. might fall in love with her husband as well. As Mann points out, both wives recognized the danger to their husbands created by the intensity of the passions felt towards them by Anna O. Yet, granting the potential dangers in such transferences if not handled properly, Mann, nonetheless, counsels that, if properly handled, the power of the erotic transference creates a splendid opportunity for its utilization for change. He says the danger and fear of it arise solely from the feelings generated by the genital excitement it occasions. But, he says, if we understand it and, therefore, perceive it as less appropriate to a more developed genital (Oedipal) level of interaction and more about a pre-oedipal relation between mother and infant, we will be able to take a more distanced, and, therefore, less aroused reaction to it. Thus, he says, it is crucial that we remember the analytic situation in terms of the analogy to reproducing, from within a transitional space, the mother-infant dyad.

The significant difference in the analogy of the mother-infant dyad to the analytic situation of psychoanalysis is, of course, that the latter has desexualized the mother's desires and, from the standpoint of the analytic situation, has separated them from the function of maternity. Thus, he says, ". . . the origins of psychoanalysis lie in the encounter of the universal sexual nature of the mind versus the analyst's attempt to extricate him or herself from its influence, to de-erotize [as it were] the inherently erotic" (p. 16). In and of itself, however, the erotic is not always transformational; for it can also be used in the service of defense and resistance as with any other psychical activity. But it always has this transformational potential. Mann suggests that the deciding factor of whether it is to be utilized in the service of growth or regression depends upon whether an individual in the analytic situation is in a transformative stage of being, ready, as it were, for growth. He offers the advice, however, that even in these circumstances, the erotic should not be actively solicited as this would be seduction; but, he says, it should not be avoided either if the patient reveals it.

The problem, Mann continues, has to do with the fact that neither patient nor therapist likes to think about the power of the erotic transference and, so, both tend to co-conspire, as it were, to deal with it in an unspoken manner. Part of this fear is fueled by the metaphors used to elucidate the analytic scene both from within and without psychoanalysis itself. He warns, therefore, that we must not fall into the trap of seeing analytic metaphors as literal and concrete facts as opposed to symbolic and abstract analogies. Thus, the therapist is *not* the patient's parent and therapy is not about just doing, by continuing, what parents have done (p. 23). On the contrary, it is the therapist's obligation to liberate the patient's capacity for new experience by freeing him or her from the limitations inscribed within his or her experience by the effects of the family scene. That is, the therapist's job is to facilitate the patient's optimal range of experience so that he or she can have more fulfilling experiences in work and love. And this is accomplished not by repeating the fixations of infantile life, but by ". . . freeing these erotic fantasies [from the constraints] of pre-Oedipal and Oedipal fixations" (p. 24). These fixations, however, have a powerful hold over all of us and, in the wrong associative linkage, can include such charged fantasies of penetrating and being penetrated that can be more disabling than empowering. The same holds true for all of one's sensuality. Thus, love, without qualification and extrication from fixation, can be a two-sided sword that, if merely enacted, can keep one mired in the past or, if understood, can have a transformational effect leading to enrichment, growth and self-realization.

Yet confusion about the erotic and its relation to 'love' continues partly because these terms have been inscribed by the linear presuppositions of the more Cartesian construction of psychoanalytic self-understanding previously discussed. In such a non-dialectical framework, these terms are arrayed as polar opposites as opposed to aspects of a dialectical unity. Granting this, though, Mann is willing to accept that there may never be a completely satisfactory definition of such a complex reality and emotion as 'love'; but he seems ready to accept Bergmann's (1988) suggestions that in satisfying and happy love there are three important salient features of 'love' that must combine: (1) a re-finding of the early love object; (2) an improving upon the old love object by finding what one has never had; and, (3) recovering, through mirroring, a certain part of one's self through the gaze of one's beloved. He remains adamant, however, that we must not distinguish in kind between the force underlying ordinary love and that underlying transference love.

The tendency to do so he sees coming primarily from Freud's vacillating between accepting transference love as ordinary love and seeing it, on the contrary, as a special and distinct, or separate, kind of love. He also has difficulty accepting Person's (1988) extrapolations on this theme. Person mentions the analytic setting as promoting regression, a sense of intimacy, and a tendency to idealize the therapist's seeming, non-judgmental knowledge. All of these elements, she thinks, go to increasing the intensity of the erotic potential in the transference and, thus, the implied suggestion that transference love is in these ways different from ordinary love. Now, whereas Mann is in

agreement with Person in her analysis of the transference situation of the analytic scene, he disagrees with her that these elements are not also present in
normal, ordinary love. In this, he cites Schafer's (1977) paper where, while
declaring transference love as transitional in nature, nonetheless, he concludes that it is as genuine as ordinary love.

Mann then turns to considering elements of hostility present in love. He ascribes it to frustration but insists that desire comes first and hostility later. In
the analytic situation, the erotic needs to be neither sexually acted out nor
simply frustrated, as the latter will induce a negative therapeutic reaction to
the therapist. Rather it should be seen, via the process of analytic interpretation, as an opportunity to expand the patient's range of emotional responsiveness. Analysts who avoid such an opportunity merely repeat old family
dynamics. Indeed, ". . . except when parents are seductive or abusive, the incestuous desire is seldom openly acknowledged or discussed and, therefore,
remains largely unresolved deep within the registers of the unconscious"
(p. 43). The point of analysis, on the contrary, is to bring such unconscious
incestuous desire to consciousness and, by so doing, liberate the patient from
the strangle-hold of fixation.

Mann notes, however, that sexualization in the transference may serve other
than sexual ends as, for instance, in the example of the need to gratify narcissistic needs or hostile wishes. Yet he remarks that sexualization in the transference is more often a disguised wish for intimacy. In noticing this, he wonders whether cultural biases may unduly influence the therapist's reactions and
interpretations of this fact by allowing confusion of the important need for intimacy in the transference for something else. Thus, for example, Mann asks,
do female analysts tend to confuse their male patient's sexual desire to be only
about "all he wants is sex" instead of recognizing it as a yearning for intimacy?
And why, he asks, have we constructed a theory of infantile incestuous desire
that is based chiefly upon the theory of male development? In connection with
this question, he notes that the feelings of horror in the case of mother-child
incest are found more objectionable, it seems, than the feeling of horror associated with father-daughter incest. He writes, ". . . the erotic mother is perceived as a threat to individuation and differentiation; her sexual desire may
voraciously swallow the child, subjecting him or her to the loss of a separate
self which will remain incorporated inside the mother" (p. 48). In the end, he
believes, though, that although there may be hostile trends within the erotic,
they are, nevertheless, subservient to its primary connecting and binding features of tenderness, affection and intimacy.

To summarize this section so far, we are reminded that both Laing and Mann
criticized a psychoanalytic self-understanding that over-emphasized mechanistic
intellectual ways of self- understanding while neglecting the richness of subjec-

tive experience in a more phenomenological and intersubjective framework. Interestingly, even though both were more focused upon the subjective and inter-subjective frame of being in a context of inter-relatedness, they could find no home within the British Object Relational School which did not approve of their inclusion of sexuality as intrinsic to the subjectivity of phenomenological experience as opposed, merely, to its being an effect of other, more underlying and distinct phenomenological substrate.

Variations of the ideas expressed by Laing and Mann have shown up in other recent journal articles by such diverse authors as Bachant (1998), Steingart (1998), Rabin (2003) and Shaw (2003). Steingart focuses on the love given by the analyst while Shaw addresses more the overall emotional impact of the analytic interaction from within the analytic situation. Both wish to distinguish 'analytic love' from transference love or countertransference. Steingart, a scholar, reminds us that, by extension, our scholarly work in the service of trying to better understand our patients can be seen as a form of love as well.

While Steingart retains the concept of analytic neutrality, Shaw believes, with the rediscovery of Ferenczi and renewed interest in interpersonalism, along with the rise and proliferation of the new intersubjectivist movements, that the trend is to more relational understandings of the process of analysis where concepts such as neutrality and abstinence are seen as neither tenable nor desirable for the best analytic results. Moreover, he feels that neutrally given interpretations by the analyst and passivity on the part of the analyst and analysand tend to stifle the potential for creating the lively emotional atmosphere he believes enhances the process. Such love, he cautions however, must be given freely and spontaneously if the analytic situation is to be an environment of trust and hope.

Steingart (1998) is not satisfied with loose definitions of love concerning aspects of the interaction between patient and analyst within the analytic situation; nor is he comfortable with a theoretical orientation that focuses primarily upon experience. Moreover, he warns from the outset against therapeutic ambition or the wish to cure. He proposes, in contrast, the idea of an epistemophillic relationship to the patient where love is expressed by the analyst's commitment to know his patient and make his patient known to himself. Making reference to such analysts as Balint and Winnicott, he says: ". . . it is the *reality* of the psychoanalytic relationship, oriented solely by the ideal "only to know" that can support early object-relation's transference experience of the most elemental sort in addition to our more customary conceptions of more Oedipal-centered psychodynamics" (p. 7). Thus, though he gives lip service to the experiential-dynamic aspects of the treatment relationship, nonetheless, by steadfastly holding to the view that analytic love is an epistemophillic (or scholarly) commitment to know, by intelligently paying devoted attention to one's patient's productions, he remains a more classically oriented Freudian analyst.

Bachant (1998), on the other hand, in writing a paper entitled, rather grandly, "Loving the Resistance: Using Resistance to Map the Boundaries of the Soul", turns to consider aspects of the concept in psychoanalysis known as "resistance". In doing so, she begins by going back to Freud's definition of the phenomenon as anything that interferes with the analytic work; most notably, when the analysand breaks off and stops his free association within the analysis. According to Freud, such resistance needs to be undone by various techniques available to the analyst that confront and, by exposing its derivatives, defeat it. About this, Freud was very vigilant to the extent, even, of noticing and complaining about what he called the "Monday morning crust" of resistance he observed in his patients following a day off from, what was otherwise, a six day treatment week for them.

Bachant, in what seems to be taking an opposite tack, wants not so much to "defeat" such resistance as, rather, to "embrace" it in order, she thinks, to "vitalize" the treatment. In comparing resistance to old habits that organize and, so, permit a sense of security for the patient, she suggests that, rather than attacking such resistance, a stance that will make the patient even more anxious, the therapist needs, instead, to reassure the patient by a stance that conveys to the patient the wish, only, of benign understanding:

> Resistance occurs on the cutting edge of the patient's development; it points us unfailingly to the place where crucial analytic work awaits our attention in the specific attitude and/or behavior that is blocking a more profound evocation, exploration or integration of psychic life (p. 127).

In presenting a more "understanding" attitude, the analyst signals to the patient a focus that is not simply about dryly interpreting internal intrapsychic conflict to the exclusion of the experiential dimension of the treatment relation; but, rather, by embracing this dimension of the treatment relationship, signals a profound respect for it and, by its explicit inclusion, allows what Bachant terms "the uniquely human hallmark of experiential adaptation" to play a significant role in the treatment. She offers this recalibration of orientation, as it were, not to the exclusion or neglect of the intrapsychic dimension of resistance, however; but, instead, cautions therapists to approach such resistance rather in the manner by which they might approach a phobic patient; that is, by encouraging the patient both to "actively" struggle with trying to overcome his or her resistance while, at the same time, allowing the analyst-analysand pair to continue in their efforts to analyze and understand it. In such a redrawing of the analytic attitude towards the patient's resistance, Bachant says that the analyst is decidedly not neutral, but, instead, becomes an aspect of the patient's auxiliary super-ego, granting the patient permission, as it were, to express his libidinal conflict without the need, any longer, to censure him or herself. She concludes this part of her presentation with the quite extraordinary insight, perhaps, that by approaching the working through of a patient's resistance in this manner, we resonate with our patients by vicarious reliving these old solutions within ourselves and, so, in a dedicated act of caring for our patients, we, vicariously, participate in a similar dedicated act of caring for ourselves.

In citing various current examples in the literature of the concern among analysts in not excluding the "experiential" dimension within the treatment relation in psychoanalysis, it is important to remember that it was Hans Loewald (2000), many years ago, who, also, in many of his writings, eloquently emphasized the importance of precisely this aspect of the treatment relation. Interestingly, Jones (2001), in noticing this about Loewald, concludes that it suggests in him a mystical vision of life which then got imported, as it were, into the psychoanalytic language of his meta-psychological pronouncements. Though somewhat of a stretch, there is, perhaps, something to this: Loewald, as we know, was very much influenced in his early formative years by Heidegger (a philosopher prone, perhaps, to 'the mystical') and was his pupil. His meta-psychological locutions often, it seems, reflects this.

For example, when Loewald says that when we self-reflect we are engaged in a "knowing-together", he is referring to an experiential state of being in which both conscious and unconscious are connected in a felt, dynamic interaction that is a form of mentation (what Heidegger might have meant by "thinking"). Moreover, Heidegger's concept of Ego is very different from Freud's. It is not, nor should it be (he thinks), the prime agency through which we understand the way reality is experienced; rather, deeper more primordial primary process sensibility needs to be incorporated into our understanding of our sense of "reality" if we are not to misrepresent, in our theoretical formulations, the vitality of the "experiential" in experience. Interestingly, and perhaps not surprisingly, this is rather reminiscent of Heidegger's notion of 'Being'; namely that underlying sense of primordial, oceanic oneness that orients us in our deepest core and makes its presence felt through a process of concealment and revealment. Indeed, for Loewald, rational life evolves, and to some extent remains parasitic upon, this earlier more global sense of 'Being' that is expressed in the experiential experience of 'being' reminiscent of Heidegger's concept of "Dasein" ("being-there") of which we have spoken previously and at length.

Importantly, Loewald's concept of narcissism is different form Freud's as well but is redolent with the same metaphysics of 'being' discussed above. Indeed, on his view, narcissistic sensibility reflects a state of primordial love that neither structures nor divides reality; but, prior to subjectivity, objectivity or language, gives to experience and mentation the quality of an underlying, undifferentiated symbiosis ('Being'). For Loewald, without access to such primordial, intuitive features of experience, life would be merely rational and "thin", impoverished and "flat"; lacking in the creativity, vitality and spontaneity so much the "heart" of living and loving.

In all of this, we have moved very far, indeed, from Freud's more mechanistic renderings of psychic life. Yet Freud was never so much a philosopher of subjectivity as, rather, more an archeologist of the mind, charting and revealing its intricate workings in ways that have inspired philosophers and scientists alike ever since; whose towering genius and fecund analyses remain, to this day, an ever protean source of insight and inspiration. Indeed, in light of his achievement and influence, it seems fair to say that nothing can ever quite be the same after Freud.

REFERENCES

Bachant, J.L. (1998) Loving the resistance: using resistance to map the boundaries of the soul. *Issues in Psychoanalytic Psychology, 20:*125–142.

Balint, M. (1968) *The Basic Fault.* London: Tavistock.

Bataille, G. (1957) *Eroticism: Death and Sexuality, trans. M. Daelwood.* San Fanscisco: City Light Books.

Bergmann, M. (1976) *The Evolution of Psychoanalytic Technique.* New York: Basic Books.

———. (1988) Freud's three theories of love in the light of later developments. *Journal of the American Psychoanalytic Association, 36:*653–672.

Binswanger, L. The existential analysis school of thought, In: *Existence.* (ed.) R. May, p. 191–213. Roman & Littlefield Publishers, 2004.

Brown, N.O. (1959) *Life Against Death.* Wesleyan: University Press.

Buber, M. (1970) *I and Thou,* trans. Walter Kaufman. New York: Charles Scribner's & Sons.

Cassirer, E. (1944) *An Essay On Man.* New Haven: Yale University Press.

Ferenczi, S. (1919) Technical difficulties in the analysis of a case of hysteria. In: *Further Contributions to the Theory and Technique of Psycho-Analysis,* p. 189–197. New York: Brunner/Mazel, 1980.

———. (1921) Further developments of an active therapy in psychoanalysis. In: *Further Contributions to the Theory and Technique of Psycho-Analysis,* p. 198–217. New York: Brunner/Mazel, 1980.

———. (1930) The principles of relaxation and neocatharsis. In: *Further Contributions to the Theory and Technique of Psycho-Analysis,* p. 108–125. New York: Brunner/Mazel, 1980.

———. (1933) Confusion of tongues between adults and the child. In: *Further Contributions to the Theory and Technique of Psycho-Analysis,* p. 156–167. New York: Brunner/Mazel, 1980.

Freud, S. (1912) The dynamics of transference. *S.E. 12*, p. 99–108.

———. (1915) Further recommendations in the technique of psychoanalysis: observations on transference love. *S.E. 12*, p. 159–171.

———. (1919) Lines of advance in psychoanalytic therapy. *S.E. 12*, p. 159–168.

———. (1930) Civilization and its Discontents. *S.E., 21:* 57–145.

Gans, S. (2000) Awakening to love: R.D. Laing's phenomenological therapy. *Psychoanalytic Review, 87:*527–547.

Groddeck, G. (1961) *The Book of the It.* New York: Funk & Wagnall.

Heidegger, M. (1962) *Being and Time.* New York: Harper & Row Publishers.

Jones, J.W. (2001) Hans Loewald: The psychoanalyst as mystic. *Psychoanalytic Review, 88:*793–809.

Kohut, H. (1984) *How Does Analysis Cure.* Chicago: The University of Chicago Press.

Langer, S. (1948) *Philosophy in A New Key.* New York: Penguin Books.

Loewald, H.W. *The Essential Loewald: Collected Papers & Monographs.* (ed.) J. Lear. Hagerstown: University Publishing Group, 2000.

Mann, D. (1966) *Psychotherapy—An Erotic Relationship.* London & New York: Rutledge.

May, R. The origins and significance of the existential movement in psychology. In: *Existence.* (ed.) R. May, p. 3–36. Rowman & Littlefield Publishers, 2004.

Mitchell, S.A. & Aron, L. (1999) *Relational Psychoanalysis: The Emergence of a Tradition.* Hillsdale, N.J.: The Analytic Press.

Ogden, T.H. (1994) The analytic third: working with intersubjective clinical facts. In: *Relational Psychoanalysis: The Emergence of a Tradition.* p. 459–493. Hillsdale, N.J.: The Analytic Press, 1999.

Person, E. (1988) *Love and Fateful Encounters: The Power of Romantic Passion.* London: Bloomsbury.

Rabin, H.M. (2003) Love in the countertransference. *Psychoanalytic Psychology, 20:*677–690.

Schafer, R. (1977) The interpretation of the transference and the conditions of loving. *Journal of the American Psychoanalytic Association, 25:*335–362.

Schweitzer, A. Reverence for life. In: *The World of Love. V.2,* (ed) I. Schneider, p. 2–24. New York: George Braziller, 1964.

Shaw, D. (2003) On the therapeutic action of analytic love. *Contemporary Psychoanalysis, 39:*251–277.

Steingart, I. (1998) The analyst's non-countertransferential love (and a footnote on hate). *Issues in Psychoanalytic Psychology, 20:*5–6.

Thompson, M.G. (2000) The heart of the matter: R.D. Laing's enigmatic relationship with psychoanalysis. *Psychoanalytic Review, 87:*483–509.

Conclusion or *"Coda"*

Having completed our explorations what, we might ask, are we left with? What can we say about love and sexuality? Who falls in love with whom and when one does fall in love is it for the sake of sexual attraction or qualities of personality? Can these really be separated? Are there any ways to predict whether any such partnership will have a happy ending? To all these questions the answers seem uncertain; for the last in particular, the answer seems to be a resounding NO. From an evolutionary point of view, we learned that romantic love was never the most important ingredient in procuring a successful mating partner. Such affairs were driven more by primitive dynamics of species viability. But in our times, people fall in love with a variety of partners for a variety of different reasons, at different times and at different stages in their lives for gratification of a variety of different needs. Certainly, even in modern times, not all selections are, to begin with, made on the basis of love; some can be very practical. For example, when a 75 year old man convinces a 30 year old woman to keep him company it might be because of his wealth, his influence or his interest in traveling to exotic places. Conversely, a 75 year old woman may convince a 30 year old man to be her escort and thus feel enlivened; the couple may even enjoy each other's company. It appears that we must distinguish between affairs formed out of purely practical considerations such as these from those that originate out of more passionate infatuation.

Although sometimes practical arrangements outlast romantic partnerships; nonetheless, we cannot predict just because the relationship is the result of purely practical considerations that it will necessarily outlast one based upon more romantic feelings. Nor can we predict who will fall in love with whom. For example, a man may prefer petite women whom he finds sexy and attractive, but this type of woman may reject his advances. Meanwhile, a career woman might prefer well-off, very masculine men, but find such to be either too sadistic or childlike. Then again, a young female college student may find herself rejected by an older man she idealizes while, on a rebound, find she has attracted the eye of one of the friends of her rejecting idol. They might become friends and, perhaps, even marry, settle down and have children. Yet none of this would have transpired if she had not been on the rebound from a man whose friend's eye just happened to catch her attention. The point is that with so many variables, no formula for predicting an affair can be arrived at. Maybe it is better we can't predict such matters and we are better off leaving such things up to circumstances and to the outcome of each man and women's unique search, marrying, when we do, out of happenstance as it were, rather than out of design. While a single life may not always be easy, particularly in later years, a contentious divorce can cause much acrimony, trauma and stress. Yet as so many marriages end in divorce, who is to say that remaining single is any worse a fate. But, hasn't it also been said that it is better to have loved and lost than never to have loved at all? And isn't 'love' a necessary condition for an examined life? And wasn't it Socrates who said that an un-examined life is a life not lived?

If we have accepted that romantic relationships are not predictable and, at best, may provide only temporary gratification until the moment when part-ners realize that somehow, initial appearances to the contrary, that: "[they] are not meant for each other," nonetheless, it is important to appreciate that often couples reach this conclusion even when it may not be valid; for whoever said that love was easy. Break-ups are all too often premature due to frustrations that could be overcome if only the partners would face their issues head on and work to salvage their relationship rather than throw in the towel in the face of the first sign of discord and conflict.

Although not paradigmatic of love relations in general, nonetheless, it might be instructive to note that, interestingly enough, office romances some-times fall in a category where, as in the above, at the first sign of a bumpy road there follows a premature break-up. For example, a somewhat typical of-fice romance scenario might well involve a man of influence in a company who, as it happens, may be either recently divorced or in the process of di-vorcing. While at first the office mate feels she has found a good catch, yet when problems with his original family arise (usually having to do with the children) she may become insecure, jealous, or possessive and make demands on her lover that he cannot fulfill. This, in turn, might likely result in conflict that could be overcome and undone with the right reassurances; but without the requisite commitment and work on behalf of both partners to salvage things, such conflict could easily also be the undoing of the relationship allowing it to end prematurely as it were. In contrast to this example, it is interesting to note that relationships beginning early on in the life cycle (as early as in high school, for example) and which continue throughout early adulthood, tend to survive much longer the thousand natural shocks that such are heir to than relationships beginning later on, even as early as college, that tend to be less resilient and often seem to suffer more the kind of problem of premature break-up as noted in the office relationship example above.

From a more global perspective, however, when we see how difficult it is for people to be happy together, the prognosis for successful love seems rather pessimistic and this rather bleak picture can leave us feeling rather sad. So, we might ask, is Brenner really right when he says that successful relationships among human beings are mostly a matter of luck or happenstance while only swans couple for life? Maybe the problem has more to do with issues arising out of relationships in the context of marriage. Maybe the picture gets a bit brighter when we focus on lasting "relationships" that are not necessarily about marriage (even though there are some marriages that seem to last even with a modicum degree of happiness). Perhaps, then, we can say something positive, and thereby feel more optimistic, if we consider what makes relationships, in all generality, last.

In all likelihood, as suggested in our example of first loves beginning as early as high school, successful relationships have to do with shared interests and growing up together throughout various stages of the life cycle. For example romances beginning in high school provide same age partners with a relationship forged at a similar stage in life and in terms of a similar environment. Such pairs have their whole life ahead of them and can dream of traversing it together, deciding, as it were, to 'get on with it' and go through the experiences of finding employment, making social friends, working towards career aspirations and planning for children. Everything of life is shared by such a couple, from teen age onward. The relationship has "legs" as it were. Even in such a closely knit couple, however, planning for a child may raise the very important issue of moving from a dyad to a triad. That is, the couple in the expectation of a child now anticipates a 'third' who can't but change the relationship between the "two" of them. If they remain sensitive to each other's feelings, and are willing to help each other with the vicissitudes of their ambivalence over such pre-emption, however, perhaps the transition from "two" to "three" may be easier to traverse than not. Yet, such an addition to the couple may well bode a rocky road ahead, for the movement from two to three always involves the activation of oedipal conflict that, as we have seen, almost certainly will lead to considerable strain on the relationship.

The wish for a child on the part of the prospective mother also involves the acceptance of a maternal role that needs to prevail in a context of "good enough mothering" whether the woman is a housewife, a career woman or a single woman. In my opinion, those who do not welcome the prospect of children are not interested in the ideas of dependence and interdependence, but, rather, seem to prefer a more regressed state of narcissistic invulnerability as a defense against experiencing self as separate but related. There are, of course, exceptions such as those women who have devoted their lives to the underprivileged or to other such persons in need (who become substitutes, as it were, for children). Also, it seems that deciding not to have children may deprive one of the sense of one's wishes and aspirations living on after one's death; also contributing to a sense of being alone without the help of one's children in times of need. The choice to exclude the having of children may, therefore, have profound effects in later life when one becomes infirmed and is in need of being taken care of.

Yet children may or may not "cement" a couple even though they are often seen as being the solution to a faltering relationship. Indeed, the wish for a "messianic child" who will rescue the couple and save the relationship may turn out to be a terrible delusion that creates even more problems for the relationship causing it to deteriorate even further. Similarly, when one partner wishes for a child and the other one refuses, there is bound to be trouble in the relationship. Of course, as analysts we know that for all the many different motives for having children, not all of them will be realistic. Yet, even just the decision to have children can create new problems as, for example, if the couple discovers fertility problems following the wish to have a child. Children, of course, are not the only sources of stress upon a couple. Indeed, it goes without saying that alcohol problems, drug abuse problems, physical illness and mental illness all contribute to the level of stress in, and therefore the viability or non viability of, a relationship.

But, turning to the brighter side and following the more optimistic approach suggested above, let us concentrate upon asking what factors we can identify that help to "cement" a relationship? We started out with the observation that partners who form relationships early in life sharing similar interests, growing up together and working toward their aspirations together may have a better chance of staying together. In a prior chapter, we speculated that men have to accept their feminine sides and women their masculine sides if they are to overcome some of the friction that is inherent in the dynamics of being a couple. We have also talked about attachment theory in respect to the coupling process. The insights gleaned from attachment theory certainly suggest much that can help us understand the art of successful relating in a relationship.

We note in such theory the claim that emotional stress and strain produce hormonal reactions that are counterproductive to the maintenance of affective states productive of emotional calm and an aura of tranquility. In a successful couple, partners help each other to stay calm and this regulatory outcome becomes neurologically imprinted. The pair are able to effect each other in a way that reduces disruptive affect. Thus, when a woman knows her partner's level of comfort and decides to forego something she had wanted for the sake of maintaining his balance in the relationship, she is helping him to remain calm and feel loved. In reciprocal fashion, at other times, she may request something for herself and he may agree to it, even though he might not have wanted to, because he remembers that she loves him.

This is not to say that couples cannot have disagreements or have varied interests. The stability of the couple and reciprocal interactions of a positive sort form the basis of the smooth regulation of affect and, hence, of more evenly modulated emotions. Under such circumstances there are few emotional disruptions and when they do occur, they are repaired quickly. On the other hand, a couple showing emotional dissonance will have many more breaks and long intervals of emotional smoldering before corrections occur and then will only tend to repeat the disruptive cycle anew. Importantly, attachment theory suggests that evenly modulated emotionally regulated couple "systems" lead to stable relationships whether couples are married or unmarried.

How do couples evolve such a comfortable system? Of major importance is the emotional distance each partner needs. Some people can be very close but then need to be apart before they can come together again. Such a gradient is different for each couple. In some instances this gradient may be different for each partner. If the degree of remove is just right, a comfortable relationship may result. Communication is of the utmost importance if such regulatory systems are to be effective. Communication may be transmitted verbally, by stance or emotionality. Words can have an almost physical impact and lead to physical arousal that may take a long time to die down. It is quite common that during intervals between outbursts partners may harbor fantasies of revenge. While we cannot prevent moods from occurring in our lives, we can take care not to hurt the partner verbally while in the grip of such a mood. Along these lines, it should be remembered that men, the weaker of the species, get hurt more easily, feel revenge longer and are prone to greater physiological disturbance from emotional upheaval.

What we call 'love,' then, is the aggregate of attraction and concern for the other: a state of 'friendship,' as it were. Such constant concern helps the couple through difficult times and regulates their emotional climate. Many people are not used to such interdependency and may shy away from it. But it can be learned if one is willing. We take this task seriously because we cannot regulate ourselves alone in a vacuum. We need another in order to make possible a life of emotional depth and stability. More profoundly, perhaps, as Plato teaches in the Symposium, without love we cannot know ourselves and, so, are unable to live a properly "human" life. In a less philosophical or, perhaps, more empirical vein, we note that without love and the internal regulation of affective balance derived from it, we tend to die and wither away emotionally, spiritually and physically. Thus, if we choose life, we cannot but choose to love. But if our love is to be "successful," we must learn the ways of love, the "meaning," as it were, of our humanity.

Index

www.ingramcontent.com/pod-product-compliance
Lightning Source LLC
Chambersburg PA
CBHW021820270326
41932CB00007B/276